Praise for *Ethics for Beginners*

"Peter Kreeft, one of the most thoughtful and prolific Catholic scholars living today, has done it again. *Ethics for Beginners* is an essential resource to introduce readers to some of the most important thinkers and ideas in this domain, as he makes the case that good and evil are real and knowable. This is an indispensable volume, coming at a crucial moment. Anyone seeking to pursue the good life and happiness most richly understood owes Kreeft a debt of gratitude."

—**O. Carter Snead**, University of Notre Dame Professor of Law, Director of de Nicola Center for Ethics and Culture, and author of *What It Means to Be Human: The Case for the Body in Public Bioethics*

"Peter Kreeft—prophet, sage, and winsome professor of philosophy— teaches readers how to unite the knowing, doing, and being of ethics against the backdrop of some of the most influential moral theorists in history, including Socrates, Buddha, Moses, Plato, Aristotle, St. Augustine, St. Thomas Aquinas, Hume, Kant, and Alasdair MacIntyre, to name a few. The cumulative goal is to make you a better person, a happy person—that is, an ethical person."

—**Matthew R. Petrusek**, Professor of Catholic Ethics, Word on Fire Institute, from the foreword

"Virtually anyone who has taken the time to look into academic discourse on ethics could understandably be scared off. You find so many different visions of the good, so much specialist jargon, so much argumentative complexity, and so many ideological agendas. Peter Kreeft has written a book that offers folks a chance to bypass these roadblocks by diving directly into accessible visions of the great masters of ethics. We desperately need nonspecialists to take ethics more seriously, not only as a tool for changing their own lives, but for the building of a new culture by those who have had their lives so changed. This book offers nonspecialists a chance to do precisely this."

—**Charles Camosy**, Professor of Medical Humanities, Creighton University School of Medicine

ETHICS FOR BEGINNERS

ETHICS FOR BEGINNERS

BIG IDEAS FROM 32 GREAT MINDS

PETER KREEFT

FOREWORD BY MATTHEW R. PETRUSEK

Published by Word on Fire, Elk Grove Village, IL 60007
© 2024 by Peter Kreeft
Printed in the United States of America
All rights reserved

Cover design by Peter Voth, typesetting by Marlene Burrell, and
interior art direction by Nicolas Fredrickson

First edition published 2020 by St. Augustine's Press
Second edition 2024

First printing, January 2024

ISBN: 978-1-68578-076-0

Library of Congress Control Number: 2023941931

Contents

IS ETHICS DEAD?

Foreword

Matthew R. Petrusek

Contemporary secular culture tends to think about "ethics" in only two ways: (1) liability-mitigating corporate training modules that instruct you what not to say and do in the workplace, and/or (2) a "break-in-case-of-emergency" box of ideas to assist in weathering a personal moral conundrum (e.g., "I just found out my friend's boyfriend might still be using his dating app—should I say something?"). In other words, secularism has reduced the role of ethics in individual and social life to a bland mush of rule-saturated PowerPoints and disposable self-help advice columns. And we have all suffered because of it.

Peter Kreeft—prophet, sage, and winsome professor of philosophy—has come to our rescue once again. His work, based in the wisdom of both natural law and revelation (another way of saying reason and faith), shows that ethics, properly defined, is neither obscure, nor rule-obsessed, nor grounded in fear, nor diminishable to mere suggestions or life hacks. Rather, ethics is about learning to be happy—truly, wholly (holy), and eternally happy, a happiness that, by its very nature, includes the generous love of both self and neighbor (see Matt. 22:39). Thus, to study ethics is to study the art of happiness; and to excel in the art of happiness, one must move from being a student to a practitioner, from knowing, to doing, to being.

That is what *Ethics for Beginners* is about: teaching readers how to unite the knowing, doing, and being of ethics against the backdrop of some of the most influential moral theories in the history of ideas. The surveys of the minds who comprise this history—including Socrates, Buddha, Moses, Plato, Aristotle, St. Augustine, St. Thomas Aquinas, Hume, Kant, and Alasdair MacIntyre, to name a few—are not only informative (though they inform exceptionally well) and not only intellectually stimulating (though each chapter leaves you thinking); they are also teleologically edifying. The critical examination of each thinker has a cumulative goal: to make you a better person, a happy person—that is, an ethical person. This goal is not a secret agenda burrowed between the lines in the text. It is the whole point of the book. *Ethics for Beginners*, Kreeft discloses, "takes a position, it argues, it tries to teach at least one very controversial idea that is unpopular among many academics, though not among people of common sense: that ethics is real, not merely ideal; that good and evil are not unknowable, subjective, or wholly relative."

Kreeft grants that many may not be willing to take this journey through the history of ideas. To all those souls standing (and sometimes booing) on the sidelines, he says, "Goodbye. Hope to see you back some day after you've gotten As in all your courses but not life." To all those, on the other hand, who are curious, or curious-adjacent, about the meaning and purpose of life and how to live it well, no matter what slings and arrows come their way, Kreeft offers this warm invitation: "Welcome to the human race and please read on."

Some advice? Don't turn this one down.

Nine Introductions

Whom This Book Is For

It's for intelligent beginners. That's why it concentrates on each thinker's "big picture," not on detailed step-by-step arguments or technical terms.

It's not for lazy, stupid beginners, and it's not for intelligent experts.

It's from 32 gurus for students; from 32 large minds for middle-sized minds; from 32 wizards for hobbits.

Since the book is for hobbits, it is not for wizards. Those who are wizards know most of the stuff in this book already, and those who think they are wizards but are not are too arrogant and self-satisfied to be good students.

Welcome, hobbits. Here are 32 ideas from 32 Gandalfs.

How This Book Is Different

This is the most boring chapter in the book. The rest of the book is about life, but this chapter is only about the book. Only an idiot would prefer a book about life to life, and only an idiot would prefer a book about a book to a book about life.

Welcome, fellow idiots.

Philosophy professors are often intelligent idiots. A philosophy professor once died, and outside the gates of heaven, God showed him a bunch of red brick buildings. It was Harvard University. "Why is that here?" the philosopher asked. "That's for you," God said. "You see, in this place everyone gets what they want the most, what they love the most. So everybody who loves wisdom the most gets to enter heaven, but those who love philosophy the most get to go to Harvard instead."

The "duh!" point of the joke is that "philosophy" literally means "the love of wisdom," not "the love of philosophy" or "the love of Harvard."

This is not the usual ethics textbook, for four reasons.

First, it is not just a classroom textbook. It is that, but it is also a do-it-yourself textbook.

Second, it concentrates only on the "big ideas," the ones that you will remember all your life and that can change your life as well as your thought. It's about the big "existential" questions, not the little "analytical" questions. And since it is about the great ideas, it uses great minds (great philosophers) and their great books. It borrows from the greatest ethical classics. It is historical rather than systematic. It's not *about* the history of ethics, it's about *ethics*; but it treats that history as a gold mine. You mine the mine for the gold. And the gold here is not the mine (history) but the minds; these gold mines are mind mines.

Third, it takes a position, it argues, it tries to teach at least one very controversial idea that is unpopular among many academics, though not among people of common sense: that ethics is real, not merely ideal; that good and evil are not unknowable, subjective, or wholly relative. Most textbooks on ethics try to be neutral on this issue, and most of them do not succeed. Their position is concealed, but operative. Mine is equally operative but not concealed.

Fourth, it focuses especially on the three biggest of all "big ideas" in ethics. To see what these are, think of the human race as a fleet of ships and life as the sea. (The image comes from C.S. Lewis.) Ethics is the ships' sailing orders. The instructions tell the ships the three things they most need to know. First and most important of all is their mission. Why are they at sea in the first place? Are they fighting a battle, or delivering cargo, or ferrying passengers to a destination, or just taking them on a pleasure cruise? Second, how should each ship stay shipshape and afloat? Third, how are they to communicate and cooperate with each other instead of ignoring each other or getting in each other's way?

The first question corresponds to the question of the *summum bonum* or "greatest good" or "ultimate end" or "meaning of life." That is an ethical question—in fact, the single most important ethical question—because it is about the simplest and most fundamental of all ethical concepts, *goodness*, about a *good* life. You will ask this question only if you are dissatisfied with getting As in all your subjects but flunking life.

The second question corresponds to individual ethics, or virtue ethics: What kind of a person should I be? This is about virtues and vices in ethics: good and bad habits of character.

The third question corresponds to social ethics: how we should behave to others, how we should treat other people. This is about justice and charity, good and bad deeds, rights and duties, both private and public or political.

Most modern ethical philosophers have these questions upside down: they spend most of their time and effort on the third question and little or none on the first. Clearly, the three questions are interrelated in a certain order of logical priority. We won't treat others well (question 3) unless we are the right kind of person (question 2). (It's also true that we won't be the right kind of person if we don't treat others well.) But the whole point of both being the right kind of person (a shipshape ship) and treating others well (cooperating with the other ships) is to accomplish the mission of the fleet (the first question). That is the most important question, the deepest and hardest question, and the one most modern ethical philosophers (except the "Existentialists") tend to ignore.

Why? Not because they are lazy or because the question is too hard for them to think about, but because most modern philosophers do not believe that human reason is capable of answering it. Most philosophers today have a weaker and narrower and less robust notion of human reason than the ancient and medieval philosophers had. So they leave that question either to religious faith or to personal feeling.

Another reason they ignore the question is because it's a question all religions claim to answer, and typically modern minds don't want to argue religion because they fear religious warfare (of which our civilization is rightly sick and of which we have seen all too much both in the past and in the present, especially in the Middle East). But that does not prove that it is not also a question for philosophy. Religion and philosophy can deal with some of the same questions without reducing either one of these two enterprises to the other if only they use different methods. Philosophy uses human reason alone, religion uses also faith in divine revelation (in Western religions) or mystical experience (in

Eastern religions). I think this ignoring of the greatest of questions by philosophers is a disastrous error and a sin against philosophy, and this book is an attempt to make up for it. After all, one of the most important things that distinguishes mankind from all the animals is that we *think* about these three questions.

The three big questions in ethics, then, are:

1. What is a truly human life? What is "the meaning of life"—i.e., its point, purpose, goal, good, or end? What is a life good for? "Why was I born? Why am I living? What's it all about, Alfie?" (A great old song and movie, by the way.) What is "the greatest good" (the *summum bonum*)?
2. How then shall I live? What kind of a person should I be? What is "a good person"?
3. How shall I treat other people?

If you are interested in these questions, welcome to the human race and please read on. If not, goodbye. Hope to see you back some day after you've gotten As in all your courses but not life.

Why Read This Book?

This chapter is meant to "sell" the book to teachers. That includes both teachers who teach others and teachers who teach themselves. (This book can be used either in school classrooms or in the classroom of the individual mind.)

Typically, there are three kinds of ethics textbooks. All three are forgettable. The point of this one is to be unforgettable. That is why it concentrates on a few "big ideas": they are the ones you will not forget but remember and use for the rest of your life, not just in an ethics class.

The most common kind of ethics textbook is an anthology of articles by mainly contemporary writers about tricky ethical issues in the modern world and modern life, or (worse) in abstract thought, like which of the four starving men on a lifeboat should the other three kill and eat? The advantage of this kind of text is that it grapples with concrete issues sometimes. But how often have you been in a lifeboat with three other people deciding which one to eat? The disadvantages are (1) that the style of contemporary philosophy articles is almost always dry and technical, and (2) that the articles are written not by great sages but by second-rate scholars, students, and teachers of philosophy like me. There *are* no great philosophers alive today. If you dispute that, please tell me their names. Who are our contemporary Platos or Aristotles? What living philosopher will be remembered one thousand years from now?

Sometimes, instead of anthologizing articles by contemporary philosophers, the author does all the work himself. But the text is still organized into *issues*, which are then analyzed and argued about logically. This is fine, and it may develop skills in technical analysis and argument (which is obviously a very good thing), but it is almost guaranteed never to change your life or even to fill your memory; ten years after reading it, nothing is big enough to remember. And this author is not a great philosopher. He may write a good book, but the great philosophers have written great books. Why prefer good books to great books?

A third kind of textbook is a history of ethics, a summary of the Great Books on ethics. This has the double advantage of being history—and therefore story, drama, narrative—and also covering the greatest philosophers. The book you hold in your hands is almost that kind of book, but not quite. For though history is a very important thing indeed, since we cannot understand our present without understanding our past, history is one thing and ethics is another. An ethics textbook should be . . . well, an ethics textbook. It may use history to teach ethics, but it should not use ethics to teach history.

This is a fourth kind of ethics text. In a single word, it gives you an *apprenticeship* to the great ethical masters—the sages, the gurus, the great minds from whom you can learn something unforgettable and life-changing. It summarizes and explains the big ideas from the big minds (and hearts), from 32 great ethical gurus at whose feet you can sit today because of that great invention of our ancestors: time travel through books.

Occasionally, instead of summarizing the guru I use his own words, because occasionally (but only occasionally) philosophers are clear and interesting writers.

The text is not long. It is just long enough to provoke original ethical thinking about the big ideas. Thus, at the end I provide an unusually "thick" set of guidelines for writing original essays on the fairly "thin" selections. The book is not designed to produce historical scholars but original, honest, clear thinkers about ethics.

Here are some of the greatest ethical thoughts of all time, by 32 of the greatest minds of all time, on the most fundamental ethical issues of all time, explained for beginners. Why settle for anything less? Why learn ethics from me when you can learn from Confucius, Buddha, Socrates, Plato, Aristotle, Aquinas, Kant, Kierkegaard, Nietzsche, and Wittgenstein?

This kind of text also has the advantage of concentrating on basic philosophical questions, on principles, rather than on particular current (and therefore ephemeral) problems. Understanding the big ideas, the basic principles, is the best way to study any science. (And ethics is a "science" in the old, broader meaning of the term: a subject organized by reason, even if it doesn't use the modern "scientific method.") You don't start physics with the problem of time travel or cold fusion, but with Newtonian mechanics. You don't start math with calculus but with arithmetic and algebra. If you have clear basic principles, you will be able to use them to evaluate ideas and problems; but if you approach problems without understanding principles, you will not be able to critically evaluate the proffered solutions to those problems. You will simply think what the author thinks, or you will simply think what you already think (or merely feel). Nothing will change. As a college professor, I find few things more depressing than the fact that well over 90 percent of all students think exactly the same predictable "politically correct" thoughts (whether left or right), even while they think they are being critical and original thinkers.

Each chapter or sub-chapter of this book concentrates on one "big idea" rather than many little ones, because that is what you will remember anyway. If you ever took a philosophy course, you know that that is exactly what you do in fact still remember now, years later. And you remember it because it changed you—it changed your thinking and, therefore, part of your life. We have less than one hundred years of lifetime to spend; why waste it on small ideas, books, and thinkers when you can invest it in big ones?

The advantage of a "Great Books" approach is very obvious: we have great friends; let's use them! If you have an important job to do, whether it's something physical, like building a bridge, or something medical, like an operation, or something intellectual, like deciding what ethical principles you will believe in and practice for the rest of your life, you are a fool not to get all the help you can get: to pick as many big brains (and hearts) as you can, to get a "second opinion" and a third, to use whatever wise friends you have. And they will mightily help you to think things through yourself, to take responsibility for your own thoughts, and to open your mind to arguments on both sides of controversies.

We all have very many good friends in philosophy. The best ones are dead. But the dead can still live! Dead writers are like ghosts: you can meet their spirits, their minds, even though their bodies are dead. In their books they left the products their minds made for us to use, just as those who built our cities left the products their bodies made for us to use.

These many philosophical friends of ours often profoundly disagree with each other. So you find not just one approach but many. Sometimes you can combine two or more big ideas, and sometimes you have to choose between them. But all of them are your friends; all of them will help you, even the ones you disagree with the most passionately. Especially them, for they challenge you to respond the most. You need reasons to disagree with someone even more than you need reasons to agree.

However, I must issue a word of warning. If you study the great sages instead of the little scribblers—i.e., if you use this book rather than any of the more typical ethics textbooks—you will be stretched and challenged; you will be bewitched, bothered, and (probably) bewildered, not only in your ability to follow an argument and in your ideological choices (which are the two things that most textbooks appeal to) but much more deeply, in your deepest values and loves, in your deepest heart (not just your feelings) as well as your mind—unless the author of this book has totally failed to be a faithful disciple of the sages that grace his pages.

Ethics is not a kind of postscript to life, like a pair of boots or an umbrella. When you were a child, your mother probably warned you not to forget your boots if it was snowing or your umbrella if it might rain. And most people today look at ethics as a kind of boot or umbrella, so that before you go out to do the really important things in life, like business or law or medicine, before you do what you do with your heart, you should briefly bother to check in with an ethicist to be sure that what you want to do is not unethical. That's ethics as a P.S. to life. (That's what most "legal ethics" or "medical ethics" or "business ethics" is composed of.) But for all the great philosophers, however radically they differ from each other on specific ethical questions, ethics is about the most fundamental, prior, and important things in life. Socrates went so far as to say that a good person does not worry much about the little things, like whether he lives or dies, but only about the one big thing: whether he is a good person or a bad one.

What Is Ethics?

Ethics is one of the main divisions of philosophy. But what is philosophy?

"The love of wisdom" is the literal meaning of the word, according to the ancient Greeks, who invented it. Inventors have naming rights over their inventions.

Most of what passes for philosophy today looks more like the cultivation of cleverness than the love of wisdom. It's neither love nor wisdom. It's not something that changes your life, and it's not something to love so much that you would die for it, as Socrates did. For him, philosophy was a kind of religion, an absolute.

What is philosophy in today's universities? It is a "department." Socrates would find that ridiculous. "The love of wisdom" is a love; is love a "department"? Does the university have a "love department"?

This book dialogues with giants, not with skittering little mouse-like minds that chatter but with big minds that think the big thoughts: Socrates, Plato, Aristotle, Jesus, Confucius, Buddha, Kant, Nietzsche. This book turns back the clock. "You can't turn back the clock" is not only a cliché; it's simply false, and it's stupid. Of course you can turn back the clock, and it's the most reasonable thing to do whenever the clock isn't telling you the real time.

I got that idea from G.K. Chesterton, a genius. That's what happens when you read Great Books: you get big ideas that challenge clichés.

So, what is ethics? I use "ethics" or "ethical" as synonymous with "morals" and "moral." Some philosophers, following many sociologists and psychologists, distinguish these two things, using "morals" to mean a person's lived values and "ethics" to mean the reflective, detached study and logical critique of morals. Still another distinction that I will not use here is the one in popular language today, especially in the media, that identifies "morals" or "morality" with sexual morality and ethics with the rest of morality—an example of our culture's unique obsession. Albert Camus, the keenly satirical atheist novelist, said that future generations will be able to summarize modern man in two propositions: "He fornicated and read the newspapers." Do not be surprised if this book expands that focus just a wee bit.

THE BASIC DIVISIONS OF PHILOSOPHY: WHAT ARE THE GREAT QUESTIONS?

Ethics is only part of philosophy, though it is the most obviously practical part, since it is about practice. What are the other parts?

Philosophy, as "the love of wisdom," can apply to anything that we want to be wise about. There is the philosophy of politics, law, education, history, science, mathematics, religion, literature, art, music, sports, sexuality, etc. You can philosophize (seek wisdom) about anything, even defecation.[1]

---

1. The philosophy of defecation? Well, consider this philosophical question: If the body and the mind are two dimensions of one and the same person, as they seem to be, is there then not a natural analogy between the way food comes in one end of our body, nourishes the body, and then goes out the other end as waste, and the way an idea comes into the mind, nourishes the mind in some way, and then in another way is also ejected by the mind insofar as it is waste? If truth is the food of the mind, can minds get constipated on truth as bowels do on food? Is there such a thing as mental diarrhea? Is that a ridiculous analogy? It may seem so, for after all, the law of noncontradiction doesn't ever begin to smell bad even after a few millennia. On the other hand, doesn't the mind critically accept only the reasonable aspects of an idea and eliminate the rest,

The five most foundational divisions of philosophy seem to be:

1. Logic and method,
2. Metaphysics,
3. Philosophical anthropology,
4. Epistemology, and
5. Ethics.

Ethics, in fact, is usually based on, or derived from, or dependent on, or at least strongly influenced by all four of these other areas of philosophy. Therefore, if you are to understand ethics, you must have at least a beginner's understanding of these other areas.

Ethics seems dependent on epistemology because what we can understand about ethics depends on what and how we can understand, and that is what epistemology is about. Epistemology, in turn, depends on anthropology because what human persons can understand depends on what human persons are, and that is what anthropology is about. We are neither apes nor angels; that is why we think differently than both apes and angels. Anthropology, in turn, depends on metaphysics because what we are, what kind of being we have, depends on what kinds of being there are; and that is what metaphysics is about. (For instance, if matter is an illusion, so are bodies, and if spirit is an illusion, so are minds or souls as distinct from brains.)

Finally, what we will discover in any field depends on what methods of discovery we use.

1. Logic and method are not really part of philosophy so much as preliminaries to it. Methods are man-made and changeable,

---

as the body is nourished only by the digestible aspects of food, and eliminates the rest?**
**What! First a serious footnote about the philosophy of defecation, and now a second footnote arguing with the previous footnote? You can't be serious; this has to be a joke. Answer: the distinction between the serious and the joke can't be serious. It has to be a joke.

but the laws of logic do not change with place or time but are the same everywhere and everywhen. For example, the law of noncontradiction does not change if you move to the People's Republic of Massachusetts or if the Republicans overthrow the Republic.

But though you have no choice in logic (it's like mathematics that way), you do have a choice in method, and the method you choose to use in order to think about the questions of philosophy often influences the conclusions you come to.

For instance, to see how method influences morality, consider a four-way conversation with Aristotle, Buddha, Marx, and Hume.

Aristotle believes, very commonsensically, that both the body's concrete senses and the mind's abstracting reason cooperate, like two blades of a pair of scissors, to find objective truth. And therefore his method combines sense experience and abstract understanding, and combines both inductive reasoning, from particular instances, and deductive reasoning, from general principles. And he applies this method to moral truths as well as other kinds of truth.

Buddha believes that no method of ordinary thinking can show you what really is—only the mystical experience of Nirvana can do that—and that his "noble eightfold path" is the best method for getting those "enlightened" eyes, which will then perceive the illusory nature of the needy, greedy self that is the source of bad behavior.

Marx believes that only a strictly materialistic, empirical scientific method can cut through deterministically conditioned class prejudice and tell you the truth; that reason is incorrigibly prejudiced by class ideology. Therefore, the first and overriding moral obligation is a social and political revolution.

And Hume believes that since "relations of ideas" and "matters of fact" never coincide, you never get certainty about anything real (only probability at best, and only by strictly empirical methods), and that since empirical methods discover no moral values, these values must be subjective feelings rather than objective truths.

You can easily see how different methods lead you to different conclusions.

2. This question of methodology is obviously closely connected to the questions of epistemology, or theory of knowledge, which deals with the questions of how knowledge works and how it should work. But methodology is also closely connected with, and has at least implicit assumptions in, metaphysics and anthropology. For instance, a method always, at least implicitly, assumes some answer to the mind-body problem. Take the following two disagreements among our four philosophers above. (a) Buddha believes that the impersonal mind can and must be freed from the illusions generated by the personal body, while Marx believes that the mind is only part of the body, or an effect of the body. (b) Hume believes that the mind cannot transcend the body, while Aristotle believes that the mind can find universal objective truths, as the body cannot, by abstracting the intelligible form (essential nature) from sensible matter.

You don't have to understand all the details of these very inadequate descriptions of different philosophies to see that the questions of ethics are entwined with questions in all the other areas of philosophy. Some philosophers (e.g., Kantians, pragmatists, and many "analytic philosophers") believe that ethics can and should be dealt with not as dependent on metaphysics or anthropology but in itself, independently, avoiding the uncertainties and disagreements found in these other areas of philosophy. Others, like most classical premodern thinkers, believe it is impossible to do that. That is one of the questions we will look at in this book.

3. Metaphysics is that division of philosophy which goes beyond ("meta") physics in generality or universality; the part of philosophy that asks questions about all reality, not just physical reality. But it's not just about non-physical reality either, if there is such a thing. Indeed, that is one of the questions of metaphysics: Is matter the only thing that is real, or is there also spirit, or mind, or soul? If so, is there a super-human spirit, or God? Another metaphysical question is whether the cause-and-effect relationship that we use in all our explanations is objectively real or is merely the way our minds have to work. Another metaphysical question is whether universals (like justice, human nature, or twoness) are real or only mental. That obviously impacts ethics because ethical values and virtues are universals. Justice, for instance—justice itself, the essential nature of justice, the quality of justice, the "whatness" of justice—is not the same as an individual just man, or just act, or just law. Is justice objectively real, to be discovered, or is it just invented and imposed by our minds?

Of all the questions of philosophy, the questions of metaphysics are the most abstract, the most removed from concrete, particular experience. But they are also the most important in the sense that it seems that our answers to all other questions depend (at least implicitly) on answers to the questions of metaphysics. For instance, imagine our four philosophers above—Aristotle, Marx, Buddha, and Hume—arguing about one of the most basic questions in ethics, namely, what is a good life?

Aristotle would say that it is a life that fulfills natural purposes or ends both of body and of soul. He can say that only because he believes there are natural purposes and that we are both body and soul. Marx would deny both of these assumptions because he is a metaphysical materialist. "Good"

for him is not discovered but constructed by political and eco-
nomic power. Buddha would base his ethics on the opposite
metaphysics from Marx's: that matter is only a projection of
mind. So he would say that the good life is one that leads to
mystical mental enlightenment and bliss, or Nirvana. And
Hume would say that we cannot *know* what "good" means
because all we can know, as distinct from believing or opin-
ing, are our material sensations and our own emotions. So he
would locate ethical goodness in our subjective feelings and
emotions. The point is that these four different ethics depend
on four different metaphysics, or on the skeptical denial of
metaphysics (Hume).

4. Philosophical anthropology asks what human nature is. Its
answers lie between those of metaphysics and those of ethics,
as can easily be seen if we continue with our imaginary conversation among the four philosophers above. What are human
beings? We are either (a) body and soul, as Aristotle says, or (b)
body only, as Marx says, or (c) mind only, as Buddha says, or
(d) unknowable, as Hume says, because reality, or being, is
either (a) both material and spiritual, or (b) material only, or
(c) spiritual only, or (d) unknowable. So all four answers in
anthropology presuppose answers to the question of metaphysics. Our ethical good is dependent on our anthropology
and our anthropology is dependent on our metaphysics.

Or is it? Hume, Kant, Nietzsche, and Wittgenstein all
deny this. Many modern philosophers are skeptical of metaphysics (and sometimes of anthropology too) but not totally
skeptical of ethics. They would deny that ethics has to base
itself on these other divisions of philosophy, but they would
not deny that there has to be an ethics. Very few of the great
philosophers have nothing important to say about ethics.
(Descartes, Hegel, and Heidegger are the only three major
examples I can think of. That is why they are not included
in this book.) For epistemology and ethics are about the

two things that nothing else in the known universe can do: rational thinking and moral choosing.

What Is Ethics Fundamentally About?

There are at least three candidates for the most important word in ethics: *good*, *right*, and *ought*. Premodern philosophers focus on good (vs. evil) as the most fundamental notion. This is a metaphysical approach. Modern philosophers often concentrate on right (vs. wrong) and rights (specified by rules or laws), or on the psychological experience of moral obligation or duty.

The word "values" can apply to all three approaches and does not presuppose either that these moral "values" are objective, metaphysical, and discovered, as most premodern cultures and philosophers believed, or that they are subjective, psychological, and created, as many modern philosophers believe.

If we begin with this word "values," we can say there are three fundamental questions in ethics: (1) what (moral) values are; (2) what their basis is (i.e., their foundation, their premises, their reasons); and (3) how they are to be applied, or their consequences. In other words, their essence, their cause, and their effect. Or, as Aristotle would say, their formal cause, their efficient cause, and their final cause.

The Relation between Ethics and Everything Else

"Everything else" includes at least (1) religion, (2) science, (3) law, (4) politics, (5) psychology, (6) art, and (7) death.

1. Ethics is an essential dimension of every religion in the world. And the world's religions, although apparently very different in their theologies, are not very different in their ethics. They all have a very high and idealistic ethics and demand the overcoming of our basic egotism or selfishness.

    As a matter of historical fact, religion has always been for most people the strongest source and foundation for ethics. Yet ethics, as a division of philosophy, relies on reason, common sense, and experience, not on religious faith. Believers in different religions will argue from different faith premises; but contrary arguments in philosophical ethics should have the same premises, derived not from religious faith but from universal human experience, common sense, and logical reasoning.

2. Ethics is a "science" in the broad, ancient sense of the word: a body of knowledge based on human reason and argued through logical principles, especially cause and effect. But it is not a "science" in the modern sense of "science"; that is, ethics does not use the scientific method, controlled experiments,

or quantitative measurement, nor does it confine itself to the empirical, the sensory. But since truth, by definition, cannot contradict truth, a true ethic cannot contradict true science.

3. "Law" could mean either (a) the laws of physical nature, like gravity, evolution, or relativity; or (b) the laws of a state, a school, a club, a team, or some other humanly invented association; or (c) the moral laws all persons ought to obey in order to be morally good persons. We know (a) by science, (b) by socialization, and (c) by conscience. Almost no one doubts that the laws of nature (a) are objective and discovered rather than subjective and created, or that the laws of society (b) are subjective and created rather than objective and discovered. The fundamental controversy in modern ethics is about the laws of morality (c). Which are they like? Are they objective and discovered by reason, like the laws of physical nature, or are they subjective and created by will, like the laws of a nation? The latter is called legal "positivism" because it holds that moral laws are "posited" by man.

4. A political system invents its own laws. They are civil laws. They differ from one society to another. If, in addition to these civil laws, there are also moral laws that are universal, then these moral laws can and should judge states and the laws of states as being morally good or bad; and these judgments can be argued about. If this is so, then there can be such things as "crimes against humanity" as well as crimes against American, German, or Turkish law. If not, there cannot. And if not, then it seems logically to follow that the Nuremberg trials of the Nazi war criminals for "crimes against humanity" were not an expression of moral justice but only of the power of the winners of the war.

5. Psychology tells us how we do in fact think, feel, desire, choose, and act. Ethics tells us how we ought to. Psychology (and also scientific anthropology and sociology) tells us what human beings are like, and that is certainly part of the basis

for what they *ought* to be like. But it is not the same thing. So a good basis for ethics would be a good knowledge of human psychology (and anthropology and sociology). And that knowledge is not necessarily from textbooks or classes. It could be from life or from great literature, which often gives us deeper insights into human character than abstract psychological theories do.

6. The moral good and the artistically beautiful are more separated in our society than in many past societies, including our own roots in classical, medieval, and Renaissance culture. We today usually expect artists to be immoral, and moralists to be unartistic and "hokey." But the two can be allies rather than enemies: great art can be a very effective moral educator (and not just by preaching "moral lessons"), and great ethics can be the main stimulus for great art. For ethics is not just about rules; it is about being more perfectly and completely human. We have said above that ethics is not just a postscript added to other things, like business, medicine, art, education, or law, a kind of "don't forget your boots and umbrella when you go out to do the really important things." It is about the really important things, about the goal and value of all these other things, about life itself. It is about "the meaning of life"—i.e., about life's value, about your good, end, purpose, or goal. It's about your *value*, not just your *values*—i.e., about the real value of you, not just about your opinions about values.

7. And therefore ethics is also about death, which puts life itself into question. Any ethical system that is silent about and irrelevant to the mystery of death is trivial. No one ever said on their deathbed, "I regret caring too much about ethics and not enough about economics."

Personal Qualifications for Understanding Ethics

Some people are skeptical of making any ethical judgments at all. They are ethical relativists, or ethical skeptics, or ethical subjectivists. They argue, "Who's to say, anyway? Who's to say what's good or bad? Who knows what's good or bad?" That is a fair and important question. But the answer to that question is very clear: the good person knows what's good or bad, and the bad person does not. Good people are wise and trustworthy, even if they are not brilliant; wicked people are not, even if they are brilliant. Everyone knows that that is true. That's one of the things we just can't not know. We all know that by experience and common sense, not clever or controversial philosophy.

So what qualifies you for ethical wisdom? It is not your ideological beliefs or scholarly expertise but your character traits.

And they come in pairs, so that it is very easy and very common to emphasize one half of each pair and forget the other half. These include:

1. adamant, committed honesty and flexible, experimental open-mindedness;
2. a hard (logical) head and a soft (loving, empathetic) heart, toughness and tenderness;

3. fair, unbiased, impersonal detachment and personal commitment and loyalty;
4. impatience (passion) and patience (maturity);
5. idealism and practicality; and
6. profound seriousness and lightness, playfulness, a sense of humor.

Nearly everyone agrees that all these qualities are desirable. The problem comes in reconciling and marrying the pairs. There is no easy gimmick.

It is like marriage between men and women that way: it's one of life's hardest tasks but also one of the most worthwhile and wonderful.

But this is a necessary task for each individual life if we are to develop wise and mature personalities. More than that, these qualities are not only necessary to have in order to become an ethically good person, but they are also necessary to have in order to *understand* ethics. You don't have to be a tree or a star to understand trees or stars, but you do have to be a good person to understand both goodness and personhood.

And it works the other way around too: the more we understand what a good person is, the more likely it is that we will become one. This means that we don't have to wait until we are saints to study ethics. We can begin by philosophizing about ethics long before we are saints. But it does mean that the saints will almost certainly understand this division of philosophy better than anyone else.

The Basis for Morality: Five Essential Options

The essential content of ethics does not vary very much, no matter what era, place, race, religion, culture, or philosophy we look at. No one but Nietzsche ever seriously called for, and no one ever succeeded in creating, a wholly new moral system, a "transvaluation of values," as he called it, in which arbitrariness, self-indulgence, egotism, cruelty, injustice, force, deliberate lying, and arrogant, sneering superiority were virtues, while wisdom, self-control, altruism, kindness, justice, reason, honesty, and humility were vices. It is psychologically impossible to experience a moral obligation to live the set of vices in the first list or to experience guilt about living the set of virtues in the second.

However, the *basis* for morality, the *reason* to be moral, the criterion of morality, is not nearly as clear. That is a question philosophers seriously disagree about. There are five basic options. They need not exclude each other. Many philosophers, such as Plato and Aquinas, affirm more than one of them. But usually, one takes precedence.

Every one of them can be found both in ancient Greece, where philosophy began, and in the modern world.

First, there is *fideism*: the idea that it is religious faith, rather than reason, that justifies moral behavior. This is taught by Euthyphro, in Plato's dialogue by that name, and by Christian or

Muslim "fundamentalists" in modern times. For them, an act is good simply because God wills it. Both are examples of Western thinkers, for whom God or the gods have a moral will; but in the East, the religious answer typically takes another, mystical form in which the absolute good and end of human life is a radical transformation of consciousness that can be called "enlightenment." (Hindus call it *mukti* or *moksha*; Buddhists call it *Nirvana*, *satori*, or *kensho*.) In this system, morality is a necessary means to that end—not because God wills it (for the God of Eastern religions has no will, usually no personality, and sometimes not even existence) but because getting egotism out of your system is a necessary preliminary for enlightenment. It is like wiping the dirt off the lens of the telescope so that you can see the stars.

Second, there is simple *hedonism*: the idea that pleasure is the supreme good and reason is to be used to calculate pleasures. Epicureanism is the ancient form of this; utilitarianism is the modern form of it. Happiness is identified with pleasure, and the moral good is whatever produces the greatest happiness for the greatest number of people. This is a "whatever" kind of moral relativism, but it is a rational and objective calculation according to the principal calculation that the end (pleasure) justifies the means.

Third, ethical *emotivism* holds that ethics is a matter of subjective feeling. We just "feel yucky" when we see something that displeases us, like a murder, and we unconsciously project that subjective feeling out onto the deed or its doer, calling them "bad." But in fact the only thing that is really bad is how we feel. David Hume, Jean-Jacques Rousseau, and A.J. Ayer teach this in modern times. This could be regarded as another version of hedonism; but utilitarian hedonism emphasizes *rational calculation* of pleasurable consequences, while emotivism emphasizes the immediate *feeling*. Pop psychology's imperative to "feel good about yourself" could be seen as a popularization of this philosophy.

Fourth, an ethics of *duty* centers on the obligation of practicing rational virtue, especially the Golden Rule (do unto others what you want done to you), simply because it is the right thing to do; and it is right because it is rational. This is the heart of Stoicism in the ancient world and Kantianism in the modern.

Fifth, the most popular position of all in most premodern cultures is an ethic of *teleology*—from *telos*, the Greek word for "end" or "purpose," and *logos*, the Greek word for "reason." Thus ethics is the study of ends. ("Ends" means objectively real good here, not just subjective desires; needs, not just wants). Thus, "the good" is our ultimate purpose or end, and "the greatest good" is the reason for lesser goods. This implies that a "natural moral law," in which human nature and its inherent laws, as known by rational wisdom (not just either feeling or calculation), is the basis of morality. The "four cardinal virtues" of wisdom, courage, self-control, and justice perfect human nature and make for both subjective happiness and objective goodness. (We might call the combination of both "blessedness.") This is taught by Socrates, Plato, and Aristotle in the ancient world, and by Aquinas in the Middle Ages, who added a religious dimension to it (that the natural law is a participation in the eternal law of God). Our modern Western civilization is the first in history in which some form of this "natural law ethic" is no longer believed by most of the mind-molders in formal (university) and informal (media) education.

For Teachers

A practical note here for teachers: there are at least three different ways to use this text in a typical thirteen- or fourteen-week course in ethics.

1. If there is too much here, just select the thinkers you deem the most important and omit or extra-credit the rest.
2. If there is too little here, supplement it with some readings in the works of the great ethical philosophers—e.g., Aristotle's *Nicomachean Ethics*, Kant's *Grounding for the Metaphysics of Morals*, and Sartre's *Existentialism and Humanism* (a great three-way contrast).
3. If there is just the right amount here, cover all 32 thinkers, one, two, or three each class day, in a two- or three-day-a-week, thirteen- or fourteen-week course. If possible, take a whole day each on Plato, Aristotle, Aquinas, and Kant, and perhaps also Nietzsche and Sartre.

Each big idea will typically have seven parts to its treatment:

1. The *question* it answers. (Nothing is duller or more meaning-less than an answer to a question you don't understand or care about.)
2. The *answer*, the point, the fundamental thesis, the "big idea" itself.

3. The *explanation* of it, in the philosopher's own words or in my summary.
4. The *arguments* for it.
5. The *presuppositions* or arguable assumptions behind it.
6. The *corollaries* or consequences, both in thought and in life.
7. The *objections* to it.

The student is invited to supply an eighth and last step: an imagined dialogue between its defenders and its critics or a comparison and logical analysis of the reasons for and against the idea. Suggestions for such essays are given in Appendix I; methods for organizing them are given in Appendix II.

One obvious format for each such essay is the following five-step analysis: (1) What is the question, issue, or problem, in your own words? (2) What is the philosopher's answer to it? (3) What is his basic reason for his answer? (4) Do you agree or disagree with his answer? (Or do you do both, by making a distinction somewhere?) (5) What are your reasons for agreeing or disagreeing with his answer and with his premises or arguments? Remember that there are only three ways to disagree with an argument's conclusion: by finding (1) a term used ambiguously, (2) a false premise (either stated or implied but needed for the argument), or (3) a logical fallacy such that the conclusion does not necessarily follow even if all the premises are true.

Students need to remember these logical structures and principles while actually writing their essays. That point may seem obvious, but I find that even intelligent students find it difficult to resist the temptation to forget them in practice and to "go off on tangents" that they find interesting, or to merely "express their feelings" instead of giving reasons.

The Oldest Ethical Teacher

How do we begin? I think we should begin a book about ethics by looking at how we all did in fact begin to think ethically, both individually and collectively as a human race. Who taught us? It was not a human person, but it was the most important teacher of all. If this teacher did not exist, none of the other teachers could teach a single ethical truth.

Religious believers will identify this teacher as God, non-believers will not. But both will have to agree that this teacher is real, because if it is not, then ethics is not possible any more than mathematics is possible if there is no such thing as a calculable number; no more than physics is possible if there is no such thing as the universe (i.e., intelligibility in matter); no more than music is possible if there is no such reality as harmony in sound; no more than art is possible if there is no such reality as beauty.

All cultures in the history of the world, except one, have believed in the reality of this ethical teacher. Our present culture, modern Western civilization, is the first culture in history whose mind-molders, for the most part, no longer believe in its existence.

Different past and present cultures have different names for this ethical teacher, different philosophical explanations for it, and different religious or nonreligious accounts of it. For instance, for some (Western religions) it is the personal character and will of the Creator God. For others (Eastern religions) it is the impersonal law of *Karma*, the moral law of cause and effect or cosmic justice

(Hinduism, Buddhism). It assumes that objective reality is more than what our senses can see and our calculating minds can calculate, even when those senses and minds are vastly expanded by scientific instruments. It means that there is a moral law that is just as objectively real as physical laws. This law is called *Karma* (justice as fate) and *Ṛta* (cosmic order) and *Tao* (the way of nature, the nature of things) in the East, *Dīkē* (justice as order) and *Logos* (truth, wisdom, reason, word) in the West. It means that just as the physical universe has walls in it, so that when you throw a ball straight at a wall it bounces back to you straight, and when you throw a ball at an angle at a wall it bounces back at an angle, so the moral universe has a kind of moral wall in it, so that when you throw a good deed at it, it comes back to reward you with good, and when you throw an evil deed at it, it comes back to punish you with harm. There is no free lunch. No one ever really gets away with anything. "You reap whatever you sow" (Gal. 6:7).

This basic notion transcends the differences among religions, and even transcends the difference between religion and irreligion. For some, it is the personal *will* of God (e.g., Al-Ash'ari and mainline Islam). For some, it is the unchangeable *character* or *nature* of God (e.g., the mainline Christian, especially Catholic, "natural law" tradition). For some, it is a kind of divine nature without a divine face or name (e.g., Stoicism, Platonism). For some, it is just the inner structure of "practical (moral) reason" (Kant). And for some, it is just objective and unchangeable moral truth without a God as its foundation (atheists and agnostics like Albert Camus, Kai Nielsen, and Antony Flew before his conversion).

The ancient Greeks called this the Logos, the law of nature. The ancient Hindus called it the Ṛta. The ancient Chinese called it the Tao, "the Way."

Even though most of the philosophers of our modern Western culture are skeptical or relativistic or subjectivistic about this Logos-Ṛta-Tao, everyone without exception in all cultures, including our own—even those who deny its reality in their philosophy—appeals to it in their use of moral language, in moral arguing. We do not merely fight like animals; we argue, we claim that we are ethically or morally right or wrong. We say things like, "Hey, get to the back of the line; I was here first," or, "How would you like it if someone called you that insulting name?" or, "That's not your suitcase; put it back!" We praise and blame, reward and punish, warn and counsel, admire and despise. And we do not act as if we thought this was mere personal feeling or private preference. We distinguish between two distinctions: the distinction between right and wrong and the distinction between convenient and inconvenient, or pleasure and pain. We do not argue about the latter, only the former. That's true of all of us, even those who are moral skeptics, relativists, or subjectivists who believe, in their philosophy, that ethics is just the rules of a game we invented, like baseball. No one feels *guilty* about changing the rules so both teams can go home after five innings instead of nine if they want to. But we do feel guilty when we cheat, rob, rape, or murder. Ethics is in fact a universal dimension of human life as life is actually lived, even when it is doubted or denied in philosophical thought. And it is a dimension that nearly everyone takes very seriously, as one of the most important dimensions of human life—in fact, usually even *the* most important one. Even if the robber feels no moral guilt in robbing, he feels a moral outrage in being robbed.

Why did I take so much time to make this simple point? Because that point, that fact, is what justifies my writing the rest of this book and your reading it.

Typically, modern philosophy (Hume, Kant, and most post-Kantian ethics) is skeptical of metaphysics and therefore grounds ethics in something else: desire (Hobbes), feeling (Rousseau), choice (Sartre), rational consistency (Kant), practicality (pragmatism), politics (Marx), or utility (Mill). Yet most of us still treat moral conscience as authoritative, even without any metaphysical foundation (God, Logos, Tao).

From a historical point of view, that is the single most momentous and important issue in ethics; and the most distinctive and unique feature of our contemporary civilization is that it no longer rests the house of ethics on that foundation.

SELECTED BIBLIOGRAPHY

C.S. Lewis, *The Abolition of Man*
C.S. Lewis, *Mere Christianity*, Book 1
Aldous Huxley, *The Perennial Philosophy*
Aldous Huxley, *Brave New World*

Four Teachers from the East

2

The Hindu Tradition: The Four Wants of Man

The oldest philosophical formulation of what is taught by this universal ethical teacher is probably Hinduism, whose roots likely go back at least five thousand years.

Hinduism is the only religion not identified with one founder. It is amazingly diverse; its four major "yogas" or "sacred tasks" (*jnana*, *bhakti*, *karma*, and *raja*) amount to four quite different religions. And so Hinduism has four ethical philosophies. But the common basis for them all is a psychology based on "the four wants of man."

For thousands of years, India has explored and mapped the details of the inner, spiritual world of the human psyche as doggedly as the West has explored the outer, material world of our planet and our universe. And India has concluded that universal human nature has four wants, or natural desires, which can be mapped in a series of concentric circles.

1. Most external and obvious is the desire for pleasure. (Freud never got further than this "pleasure principle.")
2. Then comes power (which is deeper because it includes the power over pleasure).

3. Then comes the desire to find fulfillment in more than one's own individual ego, resulting in altruism, duty, and social service.

Yet even altruism is insufficient, for it amounts to the blind leading the blind. Giving away the mere toys of pleasure and power that we have renounced does not constitute true altruism. It lacks the wisdom that knows our true ultimate good. Until we find the real meaning of life, we cannot share it with others.

4. Finally, at the heart of the human heart, if we search honestly and passionately enough, we find the (usually unconscious) desire for *mukti* or *moksha*, which means "liberation" from limitations on the three things we want most deeply: *sat, chit,* and *ananda,* or unlimited life, understanding, and joy; being, wisdom, and bliss. We taste these three foods of the soul in tiny, finite amounts, like appetizers, and our hearts are restless until they rest in the main course.

But these are the attributes of *Brahman*, the supreme and infinitely perfect God. What we really want is to shed our finite egos and become God, or one with God, or to realize that we always were God, since God is not subject to time and change. We can become ourselves only when we cease to be merely ourselves and become what infinitely transcends us. We have to shed our very selves.

How can the self escape itself? What can be done about this impossible catch-22? What is the way? The way is experience. The way is to live all ways and to learn from them all.

Unlike Western ethics, Hindu ethics does not forbid indulgence in the lesser wants, either egotistic (the first two) or altruistic (the third). In fact, it encourages this, hoping that eventually (perhaps after many reincarnations—belief in reincarnation is at the root of Hindu patience) one will learn by experience that nothing less than *mukti* will satisfy.

And then comes the supreme realization or "enlightenment": that we all already have *sat*, *chit*, and *ananda*. In fact, in the depths of our *Atman* or common soul (which is like a single undersea continent manifesting itself as separate islands to our surface consciousness), we are already *Brahman*: *tat tvam asi*, "thou art that"; *Atman* is *Brahman*. So we already have what we most deeply want: the supreme good. Really, there *is* nothing but *Brahman*, nothing in addition to *Brahman*; *Brahman* is "the one without a second." We are "inside" of *Brahman*, not outside; we are not *Brahman*'s created children, but *Brahman*'s concepts or dreams; we are not spectators of the divine play, but actors *in* it.

This mystical theology is at the basis of Hinduism's ethics. For all of Hinduism—from the caste system to the four yogas, and from ritual to philosophy—is designed to purify our desires and thoughts and thus bring us to that point of enlightenment. That realization of "the beyond within" is the greatest good, the meaning of life, the whole point of human existence.

SELECTED BIBLIOGRAPHY

Huston Smith, *The World's Religions*, "Hinduism"
Ainslie T. Embree, ed., *The Hindu Tradition*

3

Buddha
(563–483 BC):
Nirvana

Buddhism is a kind of simplified Hinduism, a kind of Hindu Protestantism.

Its founder's name was Gotama of the Siddhartha clan. "Buddha," like "Christ," is an honorific title, not a given name. It means "the awakened one" or "the man who woke up." The essence of Buddhism is an experience called "Enlightenment" or "Nirvana." "Nirvana" means literally "extinction." It is the "extinguishing" of the flame of desire and its two effects, suffering and the illusion that the ego ("I") is real.

This is a radical transformation of consciousness that cannot be defined or described in ordinary language. We can only speak of it in analogies. And the privileged analogy is in the title. In applying to himself the title of "Buddha" ("the man who woke up"), Buddha is telling us that this experience is more like the experience we have all had of waking up in the morning than anything else in our lives. (Similarly, Jesus, in telling us that "you must be born again," is telling us that becoming a Christian is more like being born than any other change in our lives.) Nirvana is the exact opposite of something dreamy; it is waking from the dream of ordinary consciousness.

Buddha did not teach that there is a God or gods, not even the Hindu supreme God, *Brahman*. He was either an atheist or an agnostic. He also explicitly denied the existence of any individual human substantial soul and therefore any individual life after death. Like most Hindus, he taught that there really is only one thing, though he did not call it God, and denied that it was a thing or substance or entity. Later Buddhists sometimes call it simply "Mind," or "Buddha-Mind," or "One-Mind," or "Only-Mind."

Despite these radical differences between Buddhism and Western religions concerning God and the soul, Buddha clearly and strongly taught essentially the same morality, at least in its negative dimension, that all other religious founders taught, which centered on the value of selfless, unselfish, or altruistic attitudes and acts. Yet Buddhism teaches that there is neither self nor other as real individual entities or substances; so it does not really teach that the self should love or respect other selves. As Chesterton puts it, it does not tell us to love our neighbors, it tells us that we *are* our neighbors. What is common to Buddha and all other religious founders is that he ruthlessly, radically attacked egotism (*taṇhā*) to dethrone it.

And the essential argument for this radical program is experience: "Try it, you'll like it." Paradoxically, only this selflessness brings peace and happiness to a self. Unless the self dies, it cannot live.

Thus, the essential *content* of Buddhist ethics is similar, at least in its negative dimension, to that of nearly all other ethical philosophers: the attack on selfishness. But the *purpose* of morality is not to get to heaven, to please God, to obey the moral law, to create a better world, or to relate to other people better. It is to be a Buddha, to wake up, to see. Only if selfishness is eradicated can we become Buddhas and "wake up" to Nirvana.

Nirvana is the "extinction" of ordinary consciousness, which is both deceptive and painful, through extinguishing the cause of this deception and pain, which is selfish desire. This extinguishing of selfish desire is done through "the noble eightfold path" of ego reduction in all areas of life. Though they are not "commandments" and they are not given by a god, their point is like that of the Ten Commandments: a program, a therapy, to change one's very self from selfish to unselfish.

Some forms of Buddhism (like Zen) reverse this cause-and-effect relationship and say that once we *see* that there is nothing to be desired, we will then stop *desiring it*. In fact, it can work both ways. The two basic Buddhist values are *prajña* and *karuṇā,* wisdom and compassion, enlightenment and unselfishness, waking up and overcoming egotism. It is a package deal—each can be a cause of the other.

Buddha summarized his whole philosophy in his "four noble truths":

1. To live is to suffer. Ordinary life is pain (*dukkha*).
2. The cause of suffering is selfish desire (*taṇhā*).
3. The way to extinguish (*Nirvana*) all suffering is to extinguish its cause.
4. The way to do this is "the noble eightfold path" of the reduction to zero of egotism in each of the eight dimensions of life.

The most important of these eight dimensions is thought. Thus, the most popular Buddhist book, the *Dhammapada*, begins this way:

All that we are is the result of what we have thought.
It is founded on our thoughts.
It is made up of our thoughts.
If a man speaks or acts with an evil thought, pain follows him as the wheel follows the foot of the ox that draws the wagon. If a man speaks or acts with a pure thought, happiness follows him like a shadow that never leaves him.

"He abused me, he beat me, he defeated me, he robbed me"—in those who harbor such thoughts hatred will never cease. For never does hatred cease by hatred here. Hatred ceases only by love [*karuṇā*, compassion]. This is an eternal law. . . .

Whatever a hater may do to a hater, or an enemy to an enemy, a wrongly directed mind will do us greater mischief. Not a mother, or a father, will do so much, nor any other relative. A well-directed mind will do us greater service.

A Western thinker makes the same point: "Sow a thought, reap an act; sow an act, reap a habit; sow a habit, reap a character; sow a character, reap a destiny."[1]

This "thought," for Buddha, is not just any thought, and not primarily rational thought or even beliefs expressed in propositions. It is a different *kind* of thought. It is an "enlightenment," a "waking-up," a "seeing."

What does that transformation of consciousness mean?

What is transformed is not so much *what* you see as *how* you see. It is, ultimately, not "you" seeing at all, it is just "seeing." It is getting the "I" out of the "I see." It is (like all mysticism) the transcending of self-consciousness.

That is the supreme good, according to Buddha. That is the meaning of life. That is also "bliss," the absence of all suffering.

SELECTED BIBLIOGRAPHY

Huston Smith, *The World's Religions*, "Buddhism"
Buddha, *The Dhammapada*
Hermann Hesse, *Siddhartha*
Nancy Wilson Ross, ed., *The World of Zen*
Tucker Callaway, *Zen Way, Jesus Way*

1. In Western religions this "destiny" is not only in this life but also after death; in most forms of Buddhism, it is not. The exception is the "Pure Land" sect, in which Buddha is a savior, an "other-power" or "higher-power" who takes souls to heaven.

4

Confucius (551–479 BC): Harmony

Buddha and Confucius are the Oriental Plato and Aristotle: the two primary teachers. As Aristotle was more commonsensical, less mystical, and more practical and this-worldly than Plato, so was Confucius compared to Buddha.

The philosophy of Confucius (Kung Fu) was mainly a system of social morality whose end was peace and harmony. His reforms were not implemented in China in his own lifetime, which was a time of culture-wide civil war ("the period of warring states"); but after his death his moral system held together in relative peace and prosperity, happiness and harmony, the world's largest culture (China) for the longest time—for over two thousand years, until Mao Zedong, history's greatest mass murderer, replaced it with a radically opposite philosophy (Marxism) based on violent revolution, class conflict, and totalitarian dictatorship. Confucius was the single most successful social reformer in human history, judged by standards of both space and time.

If there is a single concept at the heart of Confucianism, it is harmony. The word is taken from music, by analogy. Confucius was so sensitive to music that once he lost his appetite for three months because a piece of music moved him so deeply. One probably legendary Chinese emperor ruled China by music. With only minimal armies he was unable to prevent civil wars from breaking out throughout his large kingdom by force alone, so he disguised himself as a peasant and walked through his kingdom listening to the music that was sung and played. If it was happy and harmonious, he sent no troops; if not, he did. By this means, most rebellions were quelled before they erupted.

The metaphor of music works to illustrate and unify all the Confucian values, especially the five major ones: *chun tzu, jen, li, wen,* and *te.*

1. Confucius' ethics is concrete rather than abstract. It points to concrete examples rather than abstract rational principles. Its fundamental ideal is to become a *chun tzu.* This means something like a *mensch* in Judaism, one who is "magnanimous" or "great-souled" in Aristotle's ethics, or a *mahatma* in Hinduism: a morally and psychologically mature person; someone who is trustworthy and imitable; someone who has a large soul, not a small and petty one.
2. What makes one a *chun tzu* is above all *jen,* or basic benevolence and goodwill. This is the greatest of all virtues. It is close to the Christian concept of *agape.* It is a basic respect for other persons, treating others as ends rather than means to one's own personal satisfaction.
3. The means to *jen* is above all *li,* which means "propriety," or doing things the way they should be done: conforming your own acts and desires to the rules based on the nature of things rather than trying to do the reverse—i.e., trying to conform the nature of things and other people to your own will. It is the external means to the internal end of being a *chun tzu.* Confucius understood not only that proper manners of behavior issued from proper character but also vice versa. Proper manners are not the same as morality, but they are a very powerful means to teach morality. The more you act

like a *chun tzu* the more you become one. Modern Westerners tend to think of acts as *expressions* of individual thoughts and feelings, but Confucians think of them primarily as *shapers* of thoughts and feelings. Where we focus on self-expression, Confucius focused on self-discipline.

4. The most important and powerful area for improving *li* is the arts. *Wen* means "the arts of peace," the arts that promote peace, both inner and outer, both individual and social. Art is not an extra for Confucius, but a social and political necessity. Art does not exist for art's sake but for man's sake. Beauty in art is the means, beauty in the human soul is the end. *Wen*, like *li*, not only expresses the self but, much more importantly, forms us into a *chun tzu*.

5. The consequence or payoff of all these virtues is *te*, moral power, the power of moral goodness, the power of moral example, the power of the *chun tzu* to attract and motivate others. It is a kind of spiritual gravity. Power, for Confucius, is not the means to ethics but its consequence, and it is spiritual, not physical. It is the opposite of Machiavelli's principle that "all armed prophets succeed, all unarmed prophets fail." Confucius himself, like Jesus, was an unarmed prophet who succeeded in doing what he wanted most to do: the power of his teachings transformed his world.

This concept of *te* exists in Taoism and Buddhism too. The title of Taoism's basic text, *Tao Te Ching*, means "the book (*ching*) about the power (*te*) of the way (*Tao*)." In a Buddhist story, a proud samurai warrior, jealous of a pious monk's reputation, approached him and demanded his wisdom at the point of his sword. He said, "I think you are a fake, you famous wise man. What can you tell me that I do not already know?" "I can show you the gates of heaven and the gates of hell," the monk replied, "even though you are an animal and a barbarian, not a human being." The insulted warrior, enraged, took out his sword and said, "Prepare to die, you fool." "See? I have shown you the gates of hell," said the monk. The warrior, suddenly aware of his rage and the monk's fearless calm, sheathed his sword. Seeing this, the monk added, "And now I have shown you the gates of heaven." That is *te*.

Other, related Confucian values include:

1. Respect for the family and ancestors—no "generation gap."
2. Respect for the past, custom, and tradition.
3. Practicality.
4. The avoidance of extremes.
5. Modesty and humility.
6. Education as essential (Confucius is called "the First Teacher").
7. Habit and repetition in all phases of daily life as the most effective educator.
8. Moralism: deliberate moral lessons are found everywhere.
9. The interdependence of the individual and society. On the one hand, the private person and the private good exists for the common good. On the other hand, a good society is dependent not on a "system," as it is in Marxism, but on the virtue of its individual members: "If there is harmony in the soul, there will be harmony in the family. If there is harmony in the family, there will be harmony in the city. If there is harmony in the city, there will be harmony in the nation. If there is harmony in the nation, there will be harmony in the world."

SELECTED BIBLIOGRAPHY:

Huston Smith, *The World's Religions*, "Confucianism"
Confucius, *Analects*

5

Lao Tzu
(Sixth Century BC):
Nature as Teacher

Lao Tzu regarded himself as an alternative to Confucius. The two founders actually met, and Confucius did not understand Lao Tzu at all. He said, "Today I have seen a dragon." Yet most people, both in China and elsewhere, seek to blend these two different philosophies, intuiting that they both lead to gentleness and peace.

Taoism is the "way" (*Tao*) of nature. What do we mean by "nature"? Most of us today would probably answer either (1) the material universe, or (2) that part of the universe which is untouched by human hands or art. In both senses, "nature" means everything limited by matter, time, and space. Those two modern concepts of what nature is are both static and empirical (visible) answers. There is a more ancient and primitive meaning of "nature" that is also more dynamic and invisible. This ancient notion can be found in the West (in Aristotle) as well as in the East. The "nature" of a thing is the force or energy that produces its characteristic way of acting. It is the nature of birds to fly, fish to swim, fire to burn, etc. We recognize what a thing is (its "nature") by the nature of its action, by the acts it brings to birth (*natus*).

Tao (pronounced "dow"), "the Way," means three things in Taoism—or rather, it means one thing in three places or three dimensions. First of all, it is "the way" ultimate reality is. This is beyond time, space, and ordinary reason and language; it is eternal, invisible, and unsayable. The *Tao Te Ching*'s famous first line is: "The Tao that can be told is not the eternal Tao." But this single Tao is also manifested in temporal, material, visible "nature" (in the modern Western sense). And it is the guide or standard or touchstone for the good and wise human life according to "nature," which is the third Tao.

Both in nature and in life, Tao manifests its power (*te*) by apparent weakness. "The softest thing in the world rides roughshod over the strongest." Soft water, for example, conquers hard rock.

Best to be like water,
Which benefits the 10,000 things
And does not contend.
It pools where humans disdain to dwell,
Close to the Tao.

"Humans are born soft and weak. They die stiff and strong." Baby skin (full of stem cells) is stronger than dry, old skin. Women and wombs are more intimately powerful to give life than men and phalluses.

Thirty spokes join one hub:
The wheel's use comes from emptiness.
Clay is fired to make a pot:
The pot's use comes from emptiness.
Windows and doors are cut to make a room:
The room's use comes from emptiness.

The point is to "return to the uncarved block," which can be carved into anything. Abstractly put, potentiality is stronger than actuality. In the words of an old chess champion, "The threat is more powerful than its execution."

Willow trees conquer storms by bending with the wind, while oaks resist and are ripped apart. Paint with the grain, not against it. This is the solution to war. Taoist sages "do not contend, and therefore no one under heaven can contend with them." Judo is an example of this: yield to your opponent and you use his own force against him. As Lincoln said, "The best way to conquer your enemy is to make him your friend." As Jesus said, "Do not resist an evildoer. But if anyone strikes you on the right cheek, turn the other also" (Matt. 5:39). This gentleness even applies to politics: "Govern large countries as you cook small fish."

In Taoism, this lifestyle is called *wei wu wei*, or simply *wu wei*, which means "acting by not-acting." Receptivity is itself active, as any baseball catcher can tell you. If your spirit is open to the Tao of nature, it will enter you, as a man enters a woman, and give you its life, and then you will be a channel of the fundamental force of reality. In Western, Christian terms, if you begin by letting the Spirit of God enter you by faith, you will then let it out by the works of love, like a ramjet letting the air enter the engine's front end and propel it by emerging from its rear with great pressure. Our spirit is like a tube, with the wind of the Tao coming in at one end and out the other. The first and most important part of the soul is its *anima*, not its *animus*. Receptivity is not weakness but strength.

Taoism has been a powerful inspiration in all the arts in the East, largely because of the power of this psychological principle. The *Tao Te Ching* has become the second most widely read and translated book in the world, next to the Bible. Its popularity is not confined to Taoists.

It is a very simple ethic. Where Confucianism has hundreds of regulations and dozens of values, Taoism has only one. It is a remarkable contrast. Are the two compatible? Perhaps not logically, but musically. Confucian and Taoist ethics are in many ways like Classical and Romantic music; and as Beethoven perfected and synthesized both, China assimilated both of her great moral teachers.

SELECTED BIBLIOGRAPHY

Lao Tzu, *Tao Te Ching* (Addiss and Lombardo translation, the most literal)
Alan Watts, *Taoism: Way Beyond Seeking*
Alan Watts, *Tao: The Watercourse Way*
Hieromonk Damascene, *Christ the Eternal Tao*
Huston Smith, *The World's Religions*, "Taoism"

Three Teachers from the West

6

Moses
(c. 1393–1273 BC): Divine Law

Begin with Lao Tzu's sense of ultimate reality as a powerful mystery and man's highest wisdom as recognizing it and living in conformity to it—probably the two essential features of all religions. Add Confucius' focus on deeds and laws that define good and evil as expressing personal virtue and producing social harmony. Add the notion of a single God, transcendent to the universe, who created the universe out of nothing and made man in his own image and gave him explicit moral instructions about how to live through authorized prophets. Now you have Judaism.

Moses is the greatest of the Jewish "prophets." The word means "mouth" or "mouthpiece." So Moses is God's "big mouth." The prophets are God's instruments of communication to man. It was to Moses that God gave the very essence and center of Judaism, the Law. There are 613 different laws in the Jewish Scriptures, many of which are liturgical or civil laws for ancient Israel alone; but all of these are applications of just ten commandments, which are the essential moral laws for all times, all people, and all nations. Even those who do not believe they came from God acknowledge that they have been the moral foundation of Western civilization for millennia.

They are very easy to understand and very hard to obey.

They are divided into (1) obligations to God (worship no false gods, respect God's name, keep the sabbath day holy) and (2) obligations to others (honor parents, do not murder, steal, lie, commit adultery, or desire another person's property or wife).

Jesus, who was a Jew religiously as well as racially, quoted the Jewish Scriptures to summarize all ten of these commandments in two: love God with your whole heart and your neighbor as yourself.

The commandments are obvious. How are they revolutionary?

Because they united ethics and religion. They are to be obeyed for the religious reason that they are God's will, and they identify God's will as "be moral."

Religion and morality, the instinct to worship some higher being and the instinct to "do right, not wrong," are two spiritual instincts that nearly all human beings have. Even when they are denied, they are there to deny. Atheism defines itself by theism, not vice versa, and immorality defines itself by morality, not vice versa.

In the rest of the ancient world, these two instincts were not perfectly united. Typically, other cultures got their morality from philosophers, sages, kings, or lawgivers rather than from their religions. Their ethics were not necessarily religious and their religions were not very moral, as we can see from the mythologies of all polytheistic religions, whose many gods are as wildly immoral as we are. The Jews radically unified the human soul by identifying these two deep instincts, and they did this by identifying the object of religious worship (the one and only God) with the object of moral conscience, identifying the will of God with ethical behavior. Their theology was revolutionary not only because of quantity (only one God, not many) but because of quality (the character of this God was totally good, totally moral).

This did two things: it made ethics religious and made religion ethical.

First of all, it brought ethics "all the way up." The repeated formula for the reason why the Jews should obey the moral law was God: "You must be holy because I the Lord am holy." Ethics became much more important than before; it became the main point of human life, because it is the way to conform to the nature of ultimate reality. It is thus the touchstone of reason and sanity, for "reason" means first of all not cleverness but "seeing what is," and "sanity" means first of all not social conformity but "living according to reality."

Second, it brought religion "all the way down." It made religion relevant to all human lives. Not everyone believes in the same gods or the same religion, but everyone has essentially the same moral conscience. No society declares lying, murder, theft, adultery, and impiety to parents to be morally good, or declares honesty, respect, integrity, self-control, trust, justice, and love to be morally evil. So if God is behind this morality that is known by universal human reason and conscience, then God is now relevant to everyone, not just one people. The Jews are God's collective prophet to the world, his reminder of what everyone innately knows is his will: be good! He makes this will known not just by miraculous divine revelations to one people but also by a universal revelation to all through moral conscience and moral reason; therefore religion, in becoming essentially ethical, becomes also philosophical, rational, natural, and universal.

SELECTED BIBLIOGRAPHY

Huston Smith, *The World's Religions*, "Judaism"

7

Jesus
(4 BC–AD 29):
Agape Love

It is impossible to understand Jesus without understanding that he was a Jew, religiously as well as racially. He claimed to be the "Messiah," which means the "anointed one" or the "chosen one." He said, "I have come not to abolish [the Law and the prophets of Judaism] but to fulfill." ("Christ," the Greek translation of "Messiah," is an honorific title, like "Buddha," not a proper name.)

In a very oversimplified but true sense, the ethics of Jesus is to Moses what Lao Tzu is to Confucius: a focus on the single heart of ethics instead of the manifold concrete laws, duties, or commandments that are its applications.

Jesus, Moses, Muhammad, and Hindu philosophers like Shankara all answer the three greatest questions in ethics (the three points in the next paragraph) with the same answer: God. All four of them see God as the supreme good, and they assume, in preaching to unbelievers, that God can be known, at least partly, by natural human reason and conscience even apart from special divine revelation (Western religions) or mystical experience (Eastern religions). So this God is an answer to the basic question of ethics and has a proper place in philosophy and reason as well as religion and faith.

For all four of these thinkers,

1. the greatest good (*summum bonum*) is God; and therefore,
2. the kind of person we ought to be is a godlike person; and therefore,
3. the way we ought to live is the way God lives and/or the way God commands us to live.

What is distinctive in Jesus' teaching, and in Christianity, is that God is known most completely in Jesus, who is not just a prophet but the divine Son of God incarnate. What follows from this central Christian belief is that

1. the meaning of life, the *summum bonum*, and the nature of ultimate reality is Jesus; and
2. the truly human being is Jesus; and
3. the way to live and treat others is Jesus' way.

Jesus summarized all this when he said: "I am the way [question #3], and the truth [question #2], and the life [question #1]."

What does this mean?

In a single word, it means *agape* (pronounced "ah-*gah*-pay"). It means "love," but not just romantic love (*eros*) or friendship (*philia*) or instinctive affection (*storge*) but "charity," altruism, goodwill, the unselfish willing of the other person's good. Because God is *agape*, therefore we should be *agape* individuals, and all human relationships should be structured and motivated by *agape*.

In Christianity, the theological basis for the authority of this Christian ethic is Jesus' claim to divinity. But non-Christians too, who believe he was just a man, almost always believe that he was a great moral teacher. He is, quite literally, the most well-known, well-loved moral teacher in the history of the world. Neither Shankara nor Moses nor Confucius nor Lao Tzu nor Buddha nor

Muhammad has such worldwide appeal. What is the secret to his popularity?

To everyone but scholars, the answer is not obscure but obvious, because it is not complex but simple. He not only taught but also exemplified the single most precious thing in the world, the answer almost everyone knows is the best answer to the question of what is life's highest wisdom and value, the greatest good, the "meaning" or point and purpose of human life on earth. It is love (*agape*).

Instead of using any of the other common Greek words for "love" (*eros, philia, storge*), Jesus' disciples used the hitherto undefined and almost unused Greek word *agape* to designate this unique kind of love. It meant for them a love that was simple, unqualified, total, nonjudgmental, forgiving, and self-forgetful.

This love comes not just from the emotions but from the "heart," which in biblical language means the very center of the soul, as the blood-pumping organ is at the center of the body and of the life of the body. This is the pre-functional root of all the psychological functions, the non-objectifiable subject, the "I" we mean when we say "my" emotions or "my" mind or "my" will. "Will" is the closest to it because "my whole heart" means "my whole self," and the captain of that ship is not the mind (which is the navigator) or the desires (which are the sailors) but the will. *Agape* is the freely given gift of one's whole self to another, and that is why it must be an act of free will, not an emotion. Philosophers as different as Aquinas (in the *Summa*), Kant (in the *Metaphysics of Morals*), and Kierkegaard (in *Works of Love*) have pointed out that obvious fact—a fact that is *not* obvious to many people in our culture, who (largely because of the influence of Rousseau) classify love as a feeling. The logic is simple: for Jesus, love is a divine *command*, and feelings simply cannot be commanded. "I command you to feel sweet feelings of tender compassion for me" is simply silly. And Jesus was never silly. The only kind of love that can be commanded is a free choice of the will.

It is in our power to give or to withhold this love. And it can be given totally or partially. The total gift of self would be shown most clearly by martyrdom, by death. Jesus' death, thus, was a "show and tell": he showed what he told; he practiced the total gift that he preached. He gave ten pints of blood because he had ten pints to give.

This kind of love is what we all most deeply long to receive from others. It makes us the most deeply happy both to give it (try it!) and to receive it. It is also what we all know, at least subconsciously, to be our deepest and highest moral call, duty, or ideal. Thus, it unites the two strands of most modern ethical philosophy, (1) "duty ethics" and (2) "happiness ethics." The Golden Rule tells us that our fundamental moral duty is to do to others and give to others what we want them to do and give to us. And nearly everyone agrees that to be genuinely loved is what brings the most happiness to our lives. So this love is at one and the same time (1) the fulfillment of our essential moral duty, what Kant will call the "categorical imperative," which is expressed in the Golden Rule, and also (2) the fulfillment of our personal search for true happiness, which both ancient thinkers like Plato, Aristotle, Augustine, and Aquinas and modern thinkers like Mill and Freud, in very different ways, will point to as the greatest good, the end sought by all other goods as means.

The consequences of a life ruled by love, as expressed in Jesus' most famous sermon, the "Sermon on the Mount" (see Matt. 5–7), consist in a number of associated psychological qualities that we all seek: peace of mind; peace with God, with others, and with ourselves; fearlessness (overcoming even the fear of death); psychological unity and simplicity; faith (trust); detachment from greed and selfishness; and hope for the future.

The reason Jesus' ethic is so popular among non-Christians is not faith in his authority or abstract philosophical reasoning but experience: those who practice it (like Socrates, Gandhi, and the

Sufis) discover that it actually works. The happiest people in the world, in every culture and religion, are the saints.

It takes an instant to see it. It takes a lifetime to live it. Life is surprisingly complex, but its meaning is surprisingly simple.

SELECTED BIBLIOGRAPHY

The four Gospels
C.S. Lewis, *Mere Christianity*, Book 3
Peter Kreeft, *The God Who Loves You*
Peter Kreeft, *The Philosophy of Jesus*
Peter Kreeft, *Jesus Shock*

8

Muhammad (AD 570–632): Surrender

Muhammad claims to be to Jesus what Confucius is to Lao Tzu: a legal and social application of the spirit of Jesus. The ethical difference is in focus, not in essence.

The West used to use the word "Mohammedanism" for the religion of Islam. That is like calling Judaism "Mosesism" or Christianity "St. Paulism." Muhammad claimed to be only a prophet of God. He is not the center of Islam; God is. The essence of Islam is *islam*, which means literally "surrender" or "submission" to Allah. The name "Allah" means literally "*the* [one and only] God." Attribute for attribute, this is the God of the Jews and Christians. The Quran gives him ninety-nine names, with the hundredth name being unsayable. Many of the hundred are also in the Bible. But the psychological relationship to God is significantly different in Islam than in Christianity: more distant and awed, less intimate (except for the Sufis).

But this is *religion*; what does it have to do with philosophical ethics? Though Muhammad was not a philosopher, he said something philosophically significant about ethics: that its essence is *islam*, total surrender to Allah and his will.

Religious Jews and Christians do not disagree with this: it is all three religions' essential definition of a saint. The *religious* differences among the religions are about who is the greatest prophet (Moses, Jesus, or Muhammad) and about whether the definitive Word of God is the Mosaic Law, the New Testament, or the Quran. But there is also a philosophically unique ethical point in Islam about the relationship between religion and morality, between God and goodness: mainline Islam contends that an act is good *because* God commands it.

Though this is a religious answer, it is an answer to a philosophical question. The question was put by Socrates to Euthyphro in the Platonic dialogue by that name: "Is an act good because the gods will it, or do the gods will it because it is good?" Since Socrates was a monotheist, we can substitute "God" for "the gods" in his question. It is a question about the relation between religion and ethics, and thus between faith and reason (for ethics is part of philosophy, which is based on reason, not religious faith). Socrates insists that God is always rational and moral and implies that we can know this by reason. Euthyphro disagrees and defines morality in relation to God—not to God's mind or God's knowable nature but to God's *will*.

This is the teaching of mainline Islam, both Sunni and Shiite, ever since the Ash'arites triumphed over their more rationalistic opponents the Mu'tazilites in the ninth century, who ranked reason *over* faith and Aristotle *over* the Quran. (One extreme usually provokes the opposite, in a kind of seesaw reaction.) This "fideism" (or "faithism"), however, is not *creedal* orthodoxy in Islam. Islam has no creeds except the *Shahadah*: "There is no God but God, and Muhammad is his prophet." And many Muslims, especially in the West, disagree with Ash'arite voluntarism (literally, "willism") for its irrationalism.

But it is also the teaching of many modern Christian philosophers and theologians in the West. William of Ockham (fourteenth century) taught that all universals were mere names (*nomina*; thus this position is called "nominalism" in metaphysics), and therefore there was no real universal good, universal reason, or universal human nature.

Martin Luther (sixteenth century) taught *sola fide*—"faith alone" —meaning not only that faith alone, rather than faith plus morally good works, was sufficient for justification, but also that faith alone, not reason, was reliable. He called reason "the devil's whore."

John Calvin (sixteenth century) taught that fallen man was "totally depraved," and thus his natural reason was not reliable when it came to the things of God. God's absolute sovereignty trumped rational, universal ethics.

Hobbes and Hume (who were both probably atheists only pretending to be Christians for political purposes) both were skeptical of reason's ability to know universals, including moral goodness.

Kierkegaard, in *Fear and Trembling*, calls the religious faith of Abraham that made him willing to offer Isaac in human sacrifice a divinely willed "teleological [purposeful] suspension of the [rational-universal] ethical," the triumph of religion over ethics as the absolute, direct, individual relationship with God, unmediated by reason or universal principles.

On the other side, with Socrates, stand Plato, Aristotle, Augustine, Aquinas, Newman, and C.S. Lewis. They do not say that God's will *conforms* to reason and rational goodness—as a good man or a pagan god might do, as if these things judged God from above—but on the other hand, they say that reason and goodness are not contingent and changeable creations of his either, for he *is* reason and goodness. Thus, both abstract philosophy (reason) and concrete religion (faith) can "go all the way up" into the eternal and necessary divine nature. Like a man and a woman, they are different and yet meant to be married to each other. However, this position is rare in Islam.

SELECTED BIBLIOGRAPHY

Huston Smith, *The World's Religions*, "Islam"

Robert R. Reilly, *The Closing of the Muslim Mind*

Peter Kreeft, *Between Allah & Jesus*

Three Classic Greek Founders
of Philosophy

9

Socrates
(470–399 BC):
"Know Thyself"

No mere philosopher in history has ever made more of a difference than Socrates. No one ever changed the face of philosophy more. Compared to Socrates, all previous philosophers were very small children. They are all lumped together as "pre-Socratics." Socrates is truly the father of philosophy.

The Socratic revolution in philosophy consisted in two main things. First, Socrates turned the attention of philosophy to ethics. The pre-Socratic philosophers were all primarily concerned with cosmology, with the universe outside us. They were not so much primitive philosophers as primitive scientists, though their method was poetic and intuitive rather than scientific. Socrates, in total contrast, philosophized only about human life and human virtues and vices.

The second change was in method. Socrates was the first person in history who clearly knew what a logical argument was. If anyone can be said to have invented logic, it was Socrates. But he did not merely argue in monologue but in dialogue, asking a series of logical "teaching" questions like a psychoanalyst or a prosecuting attorney rather than giving answers like a preacher.

He wrote nothing. But his brilliant disciple, Plato, wrote down his conversations into "the dialogues of Plato," which remain the very best introduction to philosophy available to anyone. No one's bookshelf and no one's reading experience should be without the dialogues of Plato. They are as educationally indispensable as the plays of Shakespeare and the Bible. No one knows how much Plato "polished" Socrates' actual conversations when he wrote them up, so the line between what Socrates said and what Plato said is not clear. Only when we come to the political passages in the *Republic* and the more abstract and technical dialogues about politics, epistemology, and metaphysics that were written after the *Republic* are we fairly certain that Plato is using the now-dead Socrates as a fictionalized mouthpiece for his own views.

Socrates' personality and teaching method loom so large, and the teachings he claimed to be certain of were so few, that most modern accounts ignore the second thing for the first. Yet at least three of his ideas are life-changing and radical.

The first is that the key to moral virtue, and therefore to happiness, is wisdom. That is why Socrates was a philosopher, a "lover of wisdom." In fact, Socrates went so far as to say that moral knowledge (knowledge of the good) is virtue and virtue is knowledge; if you know the good, you will always choose it. So if you do not choose it, that is because you are ignorant. The cause of all evil is ignorance.

The second is that it is better to suffer evil than to do it. Victims are not failures; victimizers are. When we selfishly compete in the game of life, we lose more when we win than when we lose.

The third is that no evil can ever happen to a good man, either in this world or in the next—if there is a next. Like most people, Socrates *believed* in life after death. But how could he claim to *know* that this truth applied even there?

All three of these teachings sound absurd. They are commonly called "Socratic paradoxes," for a paradox is an apparent contradiction that is not really a contradiction.

The first sounds absurd because we all know people who are brilliant in their mind but corrupt in their morality, and other people who are quite unintelligent but good-hearted. We also know from our own experience that knowledge is not sufficient for virtue, for we often know clearly that we ought to do X and not Y, yet we do Y and not X. Socrates is apparently denying one of the most common experiences we all have.

The second sounds absurd because we usually fear pain (suffering evil) more than sin (doing evil). In fact, we fear sin mainly because of its painful consequences. So if Socrates is right, we are all radically wrong.

The third sounds absurd because history is full of martyrs, great and small. Socrates himself was one! Great evils happen routinely to good people—they are misunderstood, hated, persecuted, oppressed, tortured, and killed. Socrates is apparently denying the whole dark side of history.

Yet he is no fool. What could Socrates have meant by these three paradoxes?

If we understand what kind of knowledge Socrates meant when he said that virtue is knowledge, we will not only understand Socrates and welcome him back to the ranks of the sane and trustable but also find a powerful key—perhaps the single most powerful key—to becoming a good and virtuous and trustworthy and lovable human being. He meant by "knowledge" what Newman called "real assent" as distinct from "notional assent." He did not mean cleverness, nor did he mean information. He meant wisdom. And by wisdom he meant *understanding*, a true mental vision of the good, seeing how beautiful, how attractive, a morally good person and a morally good life are. If we see this, we will fall in love with it; and if we fall in love with it, we will pursue it with passion; and if we pursue it with passion, we will attain it, or at least come ever closer and closer to it. If Romeo saw virtue as something like Juliet, he would forsake everything else and marry it as he did her.

Perhaps Socrates oversimplifies here. But even an oversimplification can be an instructive thought experiment, at least. Think of his point this way: religious Jews, Christians, and Muslims believe that in heaven, or paradise, we will be morally perfect without losing our humanity or our free choice. We will be free to choose, but we will never sin. How is this possible? By the wisdom of a "beatific vision" of the perfect good in God that makes temptation impossible. Once you fall in love with God, you become wise, you see; and then you cannot even be tempted to sin. Apply this to the present life now. If only the thief was wise enough to clearly see the good of self-control and self-discipline as the honorable and beautiful thing it is and to see the evil of being a thief as the ugly thing it is; if he saw the relative value of his own soul versus the money he was about to steal; if he identified his self not with his wallet but with his soul; he then would no more steal money than he would steal mud. Thus, the more we cultivate this wisdom, the more we cultivate our own goodness and consequent happiness. As Buddha said, "What we are is determined by what we think."

What Socrates meant by his second paradox was essentially the same thing that another radical moral teacher meant when he said: "What does it profit a man to gain the whole world and lose his own soul?" If we truly knew ourselves, knew what we essentially are—namely, a person, a self, a soul, a mind, a will, not a mass of chemicals and animal instincts—we would instantly see this truth. Souls—persons—are worth more than worlds, more than galaxies. That's why Socrates thought it was so important to obey the great commandment of the god of the Delphic oracle: over his temple door was written "know thyself" (*Gnothi seauton*; later, *nosce te ipsum* in Latin).

All physical harm we do to another is also spiritual harm done to ourselves. And since the essence of the self is spirit, not body, this is the essential meaning of harm and help, evil and good.

Even if Socrates' neglect of the body is a mistake (we don't just *have* bodies as we have clothes; we *are* bodies as well as souls), it is a relatively small one compared with the mistake we usually make, sacrificing some long-range good of our own soul for some short-range good of our body, sacrificing *who we are* for *what we get* (wealth) or *how we feel* (pleasure).

Once again, it all depends on wisdom, on what we see when we look at ourselves. Do we see shapes and colors or do we see a person? Do we see a machine made of meat or a mind and a will? Do we see the heart that pumps blood or the heart that loves? Do we see only with the eye or with the mind? The mind's eye is an "I." Eyes see only eyes, but "I"s see "I"s. Know thyself!

The third paradox (that no evil can happen to a good man) follows from the same premise, the answer to the great puzzle of "know thyself." The self is the soul, not the body. Others can harm your body, but only you can harm your soul, your mind and will, your wisdom and virtue. Therefore, the martyr, like Socrates, can pity rather than fear the fools who are killing him, because the fools are really killing themselves more than they are killing the martyr. Socrates is a good man, and evil and unjust men are killing him, and death is harm; yet in the middle of this situation he seems to deny that this evil can ever exist! He solves the old puzzle of "why bad things happen to good people" by claiming that they never do! He says in the *Apology* that it is simply *impossible* for a good man ever to be harmed by a bad one. This is made impossible not by the changeable law (*nomos*, "norm") of man but by the unchangeable laws of the essential nature of things, the *Logos*. The connection is tight and the argument is logical: if you "know thyself" to be a soul, you understand that others can only harm your body; it is you alone who can harm your soul. For the evils of the soul are not death (for the soul is immortal) or disease or imprisonment or torture (those are evils to the body) but folly and vice in place of wisdom and virtue; and you, not anyone else, are responsible for your own choices between rational wisdom and folly and between moral vice and virtue. The more we understand

and live Socrates' three paradoxes, the more like Socrates himself we become.

It will be this notion of eternal laws (e.g., that justice is always profitable) based on eternal essences (e.g., the essential, unchangeable nature of justice itself) that Plato will erect into the most famous and controversial theory in the history of philosophy, the "theory of Ideas" or "theory of Forms."

SELECTED BIBLIOGRAPHY

Instead of reading books about Socrates, read Plato's dialogues (especially the *Euthyphro, Apology, Crito, Phaedo, Gorgias,* and *Symposium*).

After reading Socrates (not before), read my *Philosophy 101 by Socrates: An Introduction to Philosophy via Plato's "Apology."*

10

Plato
(427–347 BC):
Socrates Systematized

SOCRATES' WISDOM POLITICIZED

Plato is to Socrates what Jesus' disciples were to Jesus: he (1) wrote down Socrates' conversations (like Jesus, Socrates wrote nothing), and he (2) provided for them an intellectual frame, an interpretation, a justification, and a philosophical foundation.

Plato's ethical dialogues include the *Apology* (a defense of philosophy and of Socrates), the *Republic* (Plato's application of Socrates' ethics to politics), and many dialogues about specific ethical virtues, such as patriotism (*Crito*), moderation (*Charmides*), friendship (*Lysis*), courage (*Laches*), justice (*Republic*), love (*Symposium*), and piety (*Euthyphro*). The *Gorgias* is about the Socratic paradox that it is better to suffer wrong than to do it. The *Protagoras* is about the Socratic paradox that evil is ignorance. And the *Apology* is a justification for the Socratic paradox that no evil can happen to a good man.

We can look at the relationship between Socrates and Plato in two ways.

On the one hand, Plato applied Socrates' principles to politics, as Socrates never did. Thus, Plato drew out what he thought were the political corollaries or consequences of Socrates' ethical principles. For instance, there were three powers in the soul and three components to justice in the soul (wisdom in the mind, courage in the will or "spirited part," and self-control or moderation in the desires); therefore, there should be three corresponding classes in the just state: the philosopher-kings, the soldiers, and the producers, or the masses.

On the other hand, Plato *justified* Socrates' ethical principles, or life-view, with a metaphysical world-view—the most famous one in the history of philosophy—centering on the Platonic "Forms." These "Forms" are the objective truths or real essences or essential natures of things, especially the moral virtues, that Socrates always sought in his dialogues. Each dialogue begins with the question "What is . . . ?" It is a quest for a real definition of a necessary and unchangeable essence, not just a nominal definition, which is only an observation of how people in one culture and time use words.

Whether human virtues and human nature itself have such an unchangeable essence, and if so whether it is knowable, and if so whether philosophizing by the Socratic method is the way to know it, are three questions that still divide philosophers today as they did in ancient Athens. Gorgias the Sophist famously denied all three meanings of *logos* when he said that (1) there is no timeless truth; (2) even if there were, we could not know it; and (3) even if we could know it, we could not communicate it.

Politics was even more important to the ancient Athenians than it is for us moderns. To most Athenians, it did not have the reputation of being a dirty business in which you could succeed only by selling your soul. It was essentially social ethics, or morality applied to the whole community rather than the individual. Yet Socrates never entered politics, either with his body or with his speech. After his death, Plato wrote his masterpiece, the *Republic*, imagining what Socrates would have said if he had. He imagined an ideally just state headed by a "philosopher-king" with an ideally just soul. Obviously, this is Socrates himself.

What Socrates would have said had he lived to read the *Republic*, no one knows. (1) He certainly would have agreed with its final conclusion, that justice (which to Plato included wisdom and courage and moderation) was always more "profitable" than injustice—i.e., that it infallibly led to happiness, for states as well as individuals. For according to both Socrates and Plato, justice was to the soul what health was to the body. (2) And he certainly would have agreed with Plato's point that the most important public cornerstone of a good (i.e., just and happy) society is the education of its leaders, especially their moral and philosophical education. Plato *invented* university education; the world's first university was his "Academy," which lasted seven hundred years, and all "academic" institutions today are named after it. (3) But there is no evidence that Socrates would have approved the benevolent dictatorship or semi-totalitarian political class system that Plato called for in his *Republic* as the best means to that end. (However, Plato explicitly said that it was just an ideal "thought experiment" to define ideal justice, not a prescription for a political order that could actually work in this world.)

On the other hand, why should there be a gap, a double standard, between ethics and politics? Politics is made by man and for man; therefore, whatever is good for man *qua* man is good both individually and socially, for man is both individual and social. If politics is not based on ethics, on the good for man, it will be based on what is *not* good for man: on power or arbitrary will.

And yet all attempts to build an ideal politics on an ideal ethics, all utopian idealisms, have failed, including (1) Plato's own short-lived attempt to institutionalize the *Republic* in Syracuse, Sicily, at the invitation of his cousin, who was the tyrant there; (2) the uniting of church and state in the Middle Ages; (3) the "divine right of kings"; (4) the supposedly divinely inspired sharia law in Islam; and even (5) the theocracy God himself established in ancient Israel.

How to reconcile the two points in the two preceding paragraphs is one of the great pressing and unsolved problems of the modern world. The most successful regimes (e.g., Confucian China and modern America) have avoided both utopian idealism and cynicism, both optimism and pessimism.

PLATONIC IDEAS:
THE OBJECTIVE REALITY OF THE GOOD

The most important point or "payoff" of Plato's "Theory of Ideas" or "Theory of Forms" is that it is his explanation and justification for the objective reality of moral values as the basis for what was later called an unchanging and objectively real "natural moral law," in opposition to the Sophists, who were moral relativists and subjectivists.

What did Plato mean by the "Forms" or "Ideas"? A Platonic "Form" is not an external, visible, material shape seen by the eye but an internal, invisible, immaterial essence or "nature" or "what" seen by the eye of the mind, by intellectual intuition. (Many modern philosophers, being nominalists, deny that there *is* such a thing as "intellectual intuition" of universal forms or essences or natures. They reduce intuition to sensation or feeling and intellection to calculation.)

If we call Plato's Forms "Ideas," we must remember to capitalize the word; we must remember that for Plato, an "Idea" is not merely a subjective or psychological *belief* or *opinion* in someone's mind but an objective essence or meaning, like the nature of Justice, or Human Nature, or Triangularity, or Gravity, on the basis of which objective truths can be known and true propositions can be made (e.g., "Justice is a virtue," or "Human Nature includes both body and soul," or "Triangularity in two-dimensional space encloses 180 degrees," or "Gravity increases with mass and decreases with distance").

Platonic Ideas can be seen as laws. But they are not the kind of laws that are "norms" (*nomoi*), laws which can be either obeyed or disobeyed, like "Do not be unjust." They are the "natural laws" (*logoi*) that all things obey. For example, "If you are unjust, you will be unhappy, for justice is to the soul what health is to the body"—which is the main point and conclusion of the *Republic*. These laws are not invented; they are discovered in "the nature of things."

Do Platonic Ideas exist, even though they are not concrete individual entities in space and time? We all admit something like them in the mathematical and physical sciences; the "laws" of trigonometry and of physics are not invented or legislated by kings, congresses, or committees. The controversial question is whether there are such laws of moral goodness too, either in particular (virtues like courage, justice, moderation, and wisdom, the "four cardinal virtues," first enumerated by Plato) or in general ("the Idea of the Good," or Goodness itself). Does the mind discover the laws of morality as it does the laws of mathematics and physics? Or does it invent them as it invents stories, sports, and works of art? Is ethics a science (that is the position of Socrates and Plato) or an art (that is the view of the Sophists)?

Modern Western civilization is the first culture in history where the majority of educators agree with the Sophists rather than with Socrates and Plato on this all-important issue. No question in the history of philosophy is more relevant to our current social situation than this one. Stay tuned to see whether Plato is right or wrong; whether we modern Sophists are headed toward a Brave New World of cultural darkness and "soft totalitarianism" or to a Utopia of "enlightenment" and peace.

The next great philosopher, Aristotle, will accept the existence of Platonic "Ideas" but deny that they exist in themselves. For Aristotle, forms like justice are the forms of just men, just states, just actions, and just laws. They are objective and universal and unchangeable, but they are not separate from particulars. We know them not by pure reason but by beginning with sense experience and then mentally "abstracting" them from the particular examples that we meet in our sensory experience. Thus, the difference between Plato and Aristotle in ethics and politics is paralleled by their difference in metaphysics (the study of what is being, of what is real) and epistemology (the philosophical study of knowing, of how we know being).

Aristotle's philosophy—in ethics, politics, epistemology, and metaphysics—is not a repudiation of Plato's fundamental ideas but a "tweaking" or correcting of them. What Aristotle has in common with Plato is much more important than what he differs with Plato about, though that is important too. The difference between Plato and Aristotle is thus like the difference between Catholics and Protestants, or between Christians and Jews, while the difference between both of them and the ancient Sophists, or the typically modern philosophers like Machiavelli, Hobbes, Hume, Rousseau, Nietzsche, and Marx, is like the difference between theists and atheists. The parallel is not accidental; Socrates, Plato, and Aristotle were monotheists, while the Sophists were atheists or agnostics. For the most natural metaphysical "place" for Platonic Forms is in the Mind of God.

THE POINT OF THE *REPUBLIC*:
JUSTICE (HEALTH OF SOUL) AS PROFITABLE

The single point that all of the *Republic* is out to prove is not first of all about political ethics but about individual ethics. The politics is just an analogy, a parallel. The point is that the thing everyone wants—namely, happiness—is attainable only through the key moral virtue: justice. The "bottom line" is that justice is always more profitable (happifying, blessed) than injustice, both to each individual soul and to the state.

People *seem* to get away with injustice, but they never do, according to Plato. For justice is the integration of all the powers of the soul, as health is the integration and right functioning of all the organs and systems of the body. The three powers of the soul, which Plato first distinguished and which have characterized nearly all systems of psychology ever since, are the intellect, the will (which he called "the spirited part"), and the desires. (Freud's revision of them are the super-ego, the ego, and the id. He ranks them in a way Plato would consider upside down.) The moral virtues that are essential to these three powers are practical wisdom in the intellect, courage in the "spirited part," and temperance, moderation, or self-control in the desires.

It is no accident that our epics almost always have three protagonists corresponding to these three powers: prophets, kings, and priests (the three divinely instituted leaders in Old Testament Judaism); Gandalf, Aragorn, and Frodo in *The Lord of the Rings*; Spock, Kirk, and McCoy in *Star Trek*; Hooper, Quint, and Brody in *Jaws*; Hermione, Harry, and Ron in *Harry Potter*; John, Peter, and James in the Gospels; Ivan, Dmitri, and Alyosha in *The Brothers Karamazov*; the scarecrow (who needs a brain), the lion (who needs courage), and the tin man (who needs a heart) in *The Wizard of Oz*; etc.

For Plato, states are mirrors of souls, since they are created by human souls. Two conclusions follow: that states follow souls both structurally and ethically. Structurally, they show the same three-part division of powers: law-making (by the "brains"), law-enforcing (by the police, the military), and law-obeying (by the masses), as a ship has a navigator, a captain, and sailors. Ethically, souls and states are also parallel because for both, justice is the key to happiness. And justice, for Plato, is the integration of all three powers with each doing its own job. It is giving to each power of the soul and each class in the state its due.

We usually think of justice as giving to each *person* what is his due or right, but Plato includes also and first of all giving to every power of your own soul what is due to it: wisdom to the intellect, courage to the will, and self-control (moderation, order) to the appetites. And this is obviously "profitable" to us, whether or not others see it and reward it. Justice comes from within, not from without, and is rewarded essentially within, not without. Plato is saying essentially what Jesus said: "What does it profit a man if he gains the whole world but loses his own soul?" In other words, the point of one of the most detailed and far-ranging philosophy books ever written (Plato's *Republic*) is the simple but often-denied moral truism that only if you're good will you be happy.

SELECTED BIBLIOGRAPHY

Paul Elmer More, *The Religion of Plato*
Paul Shorey, *What Plato Said*
A.E. Taylor, *Plato*
Peter Kreeft, *The Platonic Tradition*
Peter Kreeft, *A Socratic Introduction to Plato's "Republic"*

Aristotle
(384–322 BC):
The Ethics of Common Sense

Here are five ethical ideas from Plato that Aristotle neither simply accepts nor simply rejects, but importantly modifies because he thinks they are too extreme.

1. The first is Plato's intellectualism, or rationalism. Plato taught that evil is ignorance and virtue is knowledge; that if you really know the good, you will do it. Therefore, virtue can be taught. This is how to make people good: by teaching, by philosophical wisdom. That was the high goal of the *Republic*. (Has it worked?)

2. Because of this power of reason, Plato believed that we can prove, with clarity and certainty, major ethical truths, like justice being always more profitable than injustice, for both souls and states. (That is the basic point of the *Republic*.) Combine this point with the first one and you get the conclusion that once you prove that justice always makes you happy and injustice makes you unhappy, you will always choose justice and never injustice. So good philosophy will make you a saint.

3. Plato believed that virtue is all you need to be happy. Socrates is happy even though he is poor, ugly, misunderstood, unjustly condemned, and killed, simply because he had virtue.

4. This, in turn, is true because the answer to "know thyself" is the soul. You are simply your soul, not your body. All you need are the goods of the soul, not the goods of the body. You only "have" a body, but you "are" a soul.

5. Man is by nature wise. We are born with "innate ideas," and we only have to "remember" them; that is the point of Socratic questioning. (The assumption behind questioning is that the person questioned knows the answer. We ask, "What time is it?" when we see someone with a watch.) And if we have knowledge by nature, then we are virtuous by nature, since virtue is moral knowledge and vice is moral ignorance.

Aristotle modifies all five of these ideas of Plato:

1. For Aristotle, mind, or intellect, or reason is necessary for ethics, but it is not sufficient. Aristotle is neither a rationalist like Plato nor an irrationalist like Rousseau but a mean between these two extremes. The whole person must be trained, or habituated, including the will and the passions, which can rebel against the reason. Aristotle distinguishes intellectual virtues, which are acquired by teaching, from moral virtues, which are acquired by habit. Virtues are good habits; they are cultivated by repetition and practice. Each virtuous act strengthens the virtuous habit, and each virtuous habit, in turn, motivates and produces virtuous acts. The same reciprocity is true of vicious acts and habits.

2. Aristotle says that the amount of rational clarity and certainty we can expect in ethics is not as great as in mathematics but greater than in rhetoric or poetry. We can give good and sufficient reasons, but they are not mathematically clear or mathematically certain. For ethics deals with many changing

situations as well as some unchanging principles. Ethics is neither a "this is it!" nor a "whatever." Aristotle is neither a rationalist nor a skeptic.

3. Happiness, or blessedness, which is the supreme and complete good for man and the one thing everyone desires as an end, not a means, is not just acting virtuously but also includes sufficient external goods and freedom from debilitating pain. The main part of happiness—virtue—is under our control; but there is also another part—external goods, or the "goods of fortune"—that is not. Complete happiness is good habits plus good luck. A man like Priam (the Greek Job, the righteous, virtuous, innocent sufferer) is not completely happy if he loses all his earthly goods, even if he does not lose his virtue. (What would Aristotle make of Socrates, or the martyred saints?) Aristotle is not a materialist (for him spiritual goods come first), but he is not an immaterialist either.

4. This inclusion of material goods, in turn, follows from Aristotle's answer to "know thyself": that we are bodies as well as souls. Aristotle is neither a materialist nor a spiritualist about human nature; that is why he is neither a materialist nor a spiritualist about human needs.

5. For Aristotle, man is born neither virtuous (as in Rousseau) nor vicious (as in Hobbes and Calvin) but with a free will (he calls it "voluntariness") and is therefore open to both virtue and vice. We can only praise or blame ourselves, not society or fate or the gods, for our own personal virtues and vices. We are born with neither virtue nor intellectual wisdom but with the capacity for both. Since we are not born with Platonic Ideas, we must learn them from experience and then rise to wisdom by rational questioning, abstraction, and induction.

HAPPINESS

In the Introduction we pointed out that ethics deals with three basic questions, corresponding to the three things a fleet of ships needs to know from its sailing orders: how the ships are to cooperate, how each ship is to stay afloat and shipshape, and what the mission of the whole fleet is. And we noted that the last question is the most important because the answer to it determines the answers to the other two. Aristotle's answer to this most important of all ethical questions is happiness. Happiness is the end, the purpose, the goal, the greatest good.

What Aristotle meant by happiness was more than just a subjective feeling. It was "true happiness," or blessedness, or flourishing: the actualizing of your human potential. Thus, it is an objective end, not just a subjective one. Drugs, or crime, or revenge may make some people "happy" for a while, but that's not true happiness; that's fake happiness, or mere subjective satisfaction.

VIRTUE

If happiness is the end, or the goal, then what is the means, the road? Virtue. Virtues are good habits, as vices are bad habits. The sum of your habits makes up your character.

Habits of doing what? Rational thinking and moral choosing, the two things other animals cannot do. Thus, intellectual virtues (above all, practical wisdom) and moral virtues (above all, the "four cardinal virtues" distinguished by Plato) are the road to happiness.

So even though Aristotle includes the body in his definition of man and includes the goods of fortune in his definition of happiness, for him the soul is more important than the body. The moral choices you make, and the virtues or moral habits that these choices form, and the personal character that is the sum of these habits, are the most important ingredients for happiness. So Aristotle is much more in agreement with Plato than in disagreement.

For both Plato and Aristotle, you can't be happy unless you're good. It's the oldest moral teaching in the world. Every pre-modern moralist in every culture in the world teaches some form of it. You probably heard it from your parents when you were a little kid. Aristotle is really just Mommy's common sense in a toga.

TELEOLOGY

Here is another common-sense notion. In calling happiness (real happiness, true happiness) the end and virtue the means, Aristotle assumes that human life has a real end or purpose or goal and that we can either attain it (in various degrees) or fail to attain it (in various degrees). Since the Greek word for "end" or "goal" is *telos*, this is called the "teleological view" of ethics.

The end or *telos* is what Aristotle called the "final cause." Aristotle taught that there are four "causes" or rational explanations for anything: (1) what it *is*, or the "formal cause," or essential nature; (2) what it's *made of*, or the "material cause," or raw material; (3) what it's made *by*, or the "efficient cause"; and (4) what it's *for*, or the "final cause," its natural end or goal or perfection. Everything made is made into something, out of something, by something, and for something.

Aristotle said that everything in nature has a final cause, not just human beings, who consciously direct their actions to an end. Fire by nature moves up, and heavy objects move down; puppies become dogs, and dogs have puppies; acorns always grow into oak trees, and oak trees make more acorns. Thus, human life, which has *conscious* purposes and ends, fits into nature, which also moves in an ordered way to ends, but *unconsciously*.

Final causality is not a scientific notion. The scientific method cannot find or prove final causes, or formal causes (essences) either, only material causes and efficient causes. The medievals applied final causality to nature, and that was good philosophy but not good physical science. But many modern philosophers make the opposite mistake in refusing to apply final causality even to human life, and that is not good philosophy or good ethics. For if humanity has no real end or final cause or purpose, then life is meaningless. It is, as Macbeth says, simply "full of sound and fury, signifying nothing." And the modern mistake is far worse than the medieval one, because ethics is more important than physics. No one about to die says, "I misspent my life: I thought too much about goodness and not enough about power; too much about how to treat my friends and too little about how to conquer matter; too much about morality and too little about technology."

THE GOLDEN MEAN

If there is one idea that runs throughout Aristotle, especially throughout his ethics, it is that the true answer to most great philosophical questions is a "golden mean" between two equal but opposite extremes, both of which are errors. Common sense almost always takes such a middle or mediating position, and errors do usually come in pairs. For (as Chesterton says) there is only one angle at which you can stand upright but always at least two opposite angles at which you can fall.

Even if you never read Aristotle, you might be able to pass a test on him simply by predicting what position he would take on most issues: the middle one. You might call him "moderate to excess" or "extremely anti-extremist." I once gave a student an A for a one-sentence essay on Aristotle's ethics. The assignment was a logical critique of any one Aristotelian idea. The paper's title was "A Logical Critique of Aristotle's Doctrine of the Golden Mean." The sentence was "This is a good idea, but Aristotle carries it to extremes."

In his epistemology also, Aristotle is a middle-of-the-roader between rationalism (Plato, Descartes) and empiricism (the Sophists, Hume).

The same is true of his anthropology: man is neither a soul nor a body but both, a "psychosomatic unity," to use modern terminology.

And both his anthropology and his epistemology follow from his metaphysics, which accepts Plato's immaterial Ideas but not their "separation" from material things. Aristotle makes them the forms (nature) *of* material things. Neither matter nor form is the whole story.

This penchant for the "golden mean" is also Aristotle's key to defining each virtue. Courage, for example, is a mean between cowardice (too much fear) and foolhardiness (too little). Modesty is a mean between shyness and exhibitionism. Temperance, or moderation, is a mean between overindulgence in sensory passions and pleasures and insensitivity to them. Justice is a mean between giving and receiving either more or less than is due. Righteous indignation is a mean between a too-cool and too-hot temper. Wit is a mean between buffoonery and humorlessness. Generosity is a mean between stinginess and irresponsible prodigality. "Proper pride" is a reasonable assessment of yourself, a mean between undue humility (denying your virtues) and arrogance (denying your vices). (Aristotle never spoke of religious pride or humility as personal attitudes toward God; he was a monotheist, but a deist. His God was the distant first cause, not the God of religious relationships.)

Each virtue regulates the behavior of the body or the emotions—i.e., actions and passions. These are the matter, or raw material, of virtue. Ethics is like art, shaping and forming the raw material into a beautiful finished product. The form is always the "golden mean" between the two extremes of too much and too little. (This principle regulates the arts too—e.g., stories should not be too long or too short, music should not be too loud or too soft, etc.) The only virtue that is not moderated in this way is moderation itself.

This is not terribly exciting. But it is terribly practical and realistic.

Two principles were inscribed over the door of the temple to Apollo at Delphi (the "Delphic oracle"). One of them was "Know thyself," which was the key to Socrates' and Plato's ethics. The other was "Nothing too much," which was the key to Aristotle's.

Plato comes to a point; Aristotle is well-rounded. Perhaps the soul, as well as the body, needs to be both. Aristotle always prefers both/and to either/or, so perhaps the most complete ethic would be a both/and of Aristotle's "both/and" and Plato's "either/or," a joining of Plato's "romantic" extremism and idealism with Aristotle's "classical" moderation and realism. Perhaps life demands a dash of wildness, as some food demands a dash of hot spices. Perhaps the complete balance is between balance and imbalance. Or, in the words of an old popular song, "We're never gonna survive, unless we get a little crazy." (I think I hear Aristotle muttering, "Oh well, okay, but just a little.")

METAPHYSICS AND ANTHROPOLOGY AS THE BASIS FOR ETHICS

The idea of the "golden mean" may be the most *distinctively* Aristotelian idea in ethics, but the ethical idea that is certainly the most *important* in Aristotle, at least for our time and our culture, is the *least* distinctive ethical idea in Aristotle because it is one that he shared with almost all other ethical thinkers (except for the Sophists) in all cultures up until our own. It is the idea of "natural law" (though Aristotle never called it that): the idea that ethics is not merely a set of laws or rules or ideals that stand by themselves, but that ethics, the science of the good for human beings, depends on what human beings are, what their essential nature is, and what the natural needs of that nature are. (These include not only bodily needs like life, health, and property but also needs of the soul, such as knowledge, understanding, and friendship.)

This, in turn, depends on metaphysics. For what *human nature* is depends on what is. If matter is the only thing that is real, then the body is the only thing that we are, and therefore bodily goods like health and pleasure are the only goods. If spirit is the only thing that is real, then the body is an illusion and our nature and our needs are merely spiritual. If both are real but separate and unrelated, then our body and soul are two entities that have nothing in common in either their nature or their needs, like a ghost in a machine. Finally, if both matter and spirit are real and related as two dimensions of one human substance or one human nature rather than two, then the ethics of Aristotle follows: that we have both bodily and spiritual natures, needs, and goods, and they are somewhat interdependent.

What is distinctively modern is not any one of these four options but the idea that one's ethics need not and should not depend on one's philosophical anthropology and certainly not on one's metaphysics—because most modern philosophers have been suspicious about the possibility of metaphysics, especially since the skeptical critiques of Hume and Kant. By typically modern standards, typically premodern ethics is naïve and rests on unprovable metaphysical foundations. It is too "thick." By typically premodern standards, typically modern ethics is too "thin" and lacking a foundation in reality.

"NATURAL LAW"

Aristotle never used the term "natural law," but later thinkers like Thomas Aquinas developed a "natural law ethic" based on Aristotelian metaphysics.

Natural *physical* laws like gravity describe what does in fact happen in the physical world; natural *moral* laws prescribe what ought to happen in the world of human moral choices.

The idea of natural law presupposes:

1. that the same essential "human nature" exists in all human beings;
2. that this human nature has natural ends;
3. that this is a standard for morality—i.e., that acts are good insofar as they respect and perfect this human nature and its natural ends and needs, and evil insofar as they disrespect, pervert, or harm it. Thus, killing, lying, stealing, and adultery are wrong by nature because life, knowledge of truth, private property, and stable families are good by nature; they are objectively real needs, not just subjectively felt wants or desires;
4. that we can know all this by natural reason, in the broad, ancient meaning of "reason": wisdom, understanding, and insight, not just a high IQ; and
5. that moral laws are therefore edicts of reason, not just will, so that moral law is objective and discovered by reason, like the laws of physics or mathematics, not subjective and invented, like the laws of the state or the rules of sports.

The typically modern alternatives to these five assumptions are:

1. nominalism, which denies the objective reality of universals like "human nature";
2. scientific positivism, which denies that such things as ends or goods, which are not in principle detectable by the scientific method, are objectively real;
3. the absolute distinction between facts and values, or "is" and "ought," so that nothing that is can be the standard for anything that ought to be;
4. moral skepticism, subjectivism, or relativism; and
5. moral voluntarism or emotivism, the primacy of will or feeling rather than reason in morality.

The two main alternatives to natural law morality in modern Western philosophy are (1) utilitarianism, which says that the only moral standard is subjective pleasure ("happiness" conceived subjectively) and that whatever we foresee will cause the greatest pleasure (happiness) for the greatest number of persons is what is morally good; and (2) Kant's "categorical imperative" (absolute duty), which is essentially the Golden Rule, to always will and do to others whatever you can rationally will all others to do, since all others are to be respected as ends equal to ourselves, not used as means to our own ends.

Both of these modern systems focus on only one of the three questions we defined as crucial to morality—namely, the question of how to treat other people. They do not address the questions of personal virtue or of the supreme good. In premodern societies, if you asked your rulers what your society taught about all three of these things, you would get an answer; in modern societies, you would not. That fact is surely one of the main reasons why philosophy (in the ancient sense of "the love of wisdom") is not nearly as important today as in the past, or alternatively, why many modern philosophers no longer claim that philosophy's task is wisdom, but merely the analysis and clarification of logic and language. The computer has replaced the sage.

SELECTED BIBLIOGRAPHY

Mortimer J. Adler, *Aristotle for Everybody: Difficult Thought Made Easy* (it lives up to its title)

W.D. Ross, *Aristotle* (a more advanced, "packed," one-volume summary)

A.E. Taylor, *Aristotle* (Aristotle's Platonism)

Henry B. Veatch, *Rational Man*

Aristotle, *Nicomachean Ethics*

Sophists, Stoics, and Epicureans

Socrates, Plato, and Aristotle were perhaps the three greatest philosophers who ever lived. Our next three philosophers, one from Greece (before Socrates) and two from Rome (after Aristotle), are not usually recognized as "great," yet their ethical views are probably more popular than those of Socrates, Plato, and Aristotle, both in their own day and in ours. They are simple and easy philosophies, both to think and to live: easy to think because they are all philosophies of one basic idea, and easy to live because they are not complex, complete, and comprehensive but simple, specialized, and (to speak frankly) somewhat shallow. This is why they are popular. (If you think I am being cynical, remember how many people read trashy novels and how many read classics.)

Three Lesser but More Popular Ancient Philosophers

Protagoras
(481–420 BC):
Sophism

In nearly all of his dialogues, Plato has Socrates arguing with a Sophist. The Sophists were the first philosophers who used logical arguments about ethics, and their ethical philosophy was, in a word, relativism. Moral rules were like the rules of a sport or of a state: wholly man-made and relative to human wills. In other words, they were (1) relative to human *wills*, which made them, (2) relative to *time* and changeable, and (3) relative to the particular *place* or culture they were from and for. They were not (1) objective, (2) unchangeable, or (3) universal.

Socrates, Plato, and Aristotle could all be labeled ethical absolutists because they defended traditional "natural law" morality in all three of these ways, while the Sophists denied it. Moral relativism almost always says that morality lacks all three of these properties.

Protagoras was the most famous and successful of the Sophists. He famously summarized his philosophy by saying that "man is the measure of all things." Not God or the gods, not nature or the nature of things, but man. And not man in the sense of universal and unchanging human nature, but concrete, particular individuals who make or "posit" the laws. Thus, this position is sometimes called "ethical positivism."

Another way to put the same point is that all moral laws are social conventions. The Greek word for conventional law is *nomos*, from which we get our word "norms." The Greek word for natural law—whether in logic (like the law of identity, X=X, or the law of noncontradiction, that X is not non-X), or mathematics (like "two quantities equal to a common third quantity are equal to each other"), or physics (like the law of gravity), or ethics (like the Golden Rule, "do unto others what you want others to do to you")—is *logos*.

So according to the Sophists, the laws of your society are the highest laws. There are no higher, more universal laws that can judge a society as morally good or bad. Thus, in one sense the Sophists were against the establishment, which claimed divine or natural sanction for its laws, but in another sense they were hyper-conservatives who denied that there could ever be a moral justification for social rebellion, since there were no higher laws than society's laws. "Justice" was simply the propaganda term that was used to "sell" whatever laws were made by whoever had the power to make them; thus, literally, "might makes right."

This issue divides modern Western civilization more basically than any other today. Nearly all law schools used to teach some version of the natural law; nearly all law schools today either deny or ignore it. But polls show that most people, at least those outside media and education, still believe in some objective, universal, and unchangeable moral laws when it comes to anything outside of sex, however logically inconsistent that may be. (You might argue about that: Is sex an exception to natural law? Why or why not?)

The Sophists drew the practical consequence of their basic moral principle of relativism by getting very rich teaching people how to use rhetorical tricks to sway voters or jurors. (Athens had invented two great things: the world's first system of democracy and jury trials.) This was the Sophists' purely pragmatic "wisdom."

As Protagoras said, "What I mean by a wise man is one who can alter people's ways of judging so that what appears bad to them now will appear good to them. It is like the case of some food which appears bitter to a sick man but appears quite the opposite to a man of health. It should not be said that either of the two men is more knowing or more ignorant than the other; they are simply different. . . . My position, then, is that whatever seems right and admirable to a particular city-state is truly right and admirable, during the period of time in which that opinion continues to be held."

In other words, life is advertising and "image is everything," for there is nothing behind or above images or appearances to judge them. Socrates disagreed and assumed that in ethics as in science there was more to reality than appearance. That is why he was a philosopher, a lover of wisdom, a seeker, a questioner. The Sophists asked questions only to break people's convictions down; Socrates asked questions also to try to build them up. Each of his dialogues is an attempt to find the objective and unchanging reality behind the subjective and changing appearances.

There are at least six problems with the Sophists' moral relativism:

1. A logical problem of self-contradiction: Is relativism relative? Is the skeptic not skeptical of his skepticism? Is it really valuable to debunk the idea that values are real? Protagoras argues that "it is not possible to think what is false, because one can only think what he experiences, and what he experiences is true [to him]." But this seems to assume that we can know that we cannot know the objective truth, and thus that it *is* possible to think what is false, for the Sophists are saying that what the Sophists' traditionalist opponents believe is false (namely, that there really are objective, universal, and unchangeable moral laws). If every opinion is true, so is the opinion that *not* every opinion is true.

2. Another more psychological problem with moral relativism is that it seems to debunk and weaken the authority of conscience. If moral laws are no more than the rules of a game, why should we feel guilty about disobeying them? If we made the rules, we can remake or unmake them.

3. A psychological and aesthetic problem with relativism is that it seems to make heroism, and thus really great dramas and interesting stories, impossible.

4. A sociological problem with relativism is that it naturally weakens social bonds and thus society itself, for treating promises as really binding is the first and foundational requirement for all social bonds. If "there is nothing either good or bad, but thinking makes it so," as Hamlet says, then *why not* do whatever evil you want to do as long as you don't get caught? Without the "inner cop" of conscience, society either decays into chaos or comes to rely more and more on the outer cop of force and becomes totalitarian in order to keep order.

5. Still another problem is that the vast majority of societies, religions, philosophers, and ordinary people have always believed the opposite of what the Sophists believed. Is it likely that the vast majority of people, especially wise and good people, were so fundamentally wrong and that the small minority were right? Remember "the democracy of the dead" when you tabulate the votes.

6. Finally, an instinctive problem is that relativism seems negative and cynical and *immoral*. It takes morality not only less seriously than extreme moralists do but also less seriously than most average people do.

Moral relativists (of which there are many today, so many that some readers of this book must be among them) are invited to answer these six objections. Many modern philosophers (Hobbes, Hume, Mill, Sartre, Nietzsche) will try to do just that. They offer a more sophisticated version of the Sophists' moral relativism.

13

Epicurus
(342–270 BC):
Hedonism

In this section, we will concentrate not on Epicurus himself and the details of his thought but the issue he brings up, because that issue will recur many times later with other more famous and influential philosophers.

"Epicureanism," named after Epicurus, the ancient Roman philosopher, is attractive because it is extremely simple.

We love simplicity because it unifies our thoughts and our lives. Both our heads and our hearts need to be one in order for us to be truly one person.

That does not mean that we need to deny the pluralities and complexities of thought or life, but that we need a single page on which to draw the many lines that make up a picture, no matter how complex that picture may be. What life gives us is the page, and what we supply is the picture. We also want simplicity in two other senses: something that unifies all our choices and wills and desires and loves, and something that unifies our bodies and hands and actions.

In other words, we need a simplicity in our head (our thinking) and in our heart (our loving) and in our hands (our doing). Epicurus offers us an attractively simple ethics in all three dimensions.

Hedonism is attractive because it is intellectually simple for head, heart, and hands. (1) We all know what pleasure is, without any profound philosophical wisdom. (2) We all love it, especially bodily pleasures, and we all hate pain, especially bodily pain. (3) And we all can attain some pleasures and avoid some pains quite easily; it does not take heroic effort or sanctity.

It is called "hedonism," after the Greek word *hēdonē*, which means "pleasure." The greatest good is pleasure, according to hedonism. In fact, the *only* good in itself is pleasure. All other things are good only because they are pleasures, or parts of pleasure, or means to the end of pleasure. For instance, money is good not in itself (who wants dirty pieces of paper or metal?) but only because it buys for us goods and services that make us happy by pleasing us.

In the above paragraph, I used the word "happy" as a synonym for "pleased," and (implicitly) "happiness" as a synonym for "pleasure." That is exactly what Epicurus would do if he wrote in English. But Aristotle would not. The Greek word Aristotle used for the greatest good, or *summum bonum*, was *eudaimonia*. *Eudaimonia* has in it three assumptions that the English word "happiness" does not necessarily have and that the Greek word *hēdonē* definitely does not have.

1. Its prefix *eu-* means "good"; and Aristotle, like Plato, interprets that as meaning "morally good"—that is, not merely what pleases us but what ought to please us, what we ought to love and do. In other words, real needs, not just felt wants.
2. Its central part, *daimon*, means "spirit," which implies that *eudaimonia* is located not primarily in the body but in the spirit or soul.
3. And its suffix *-ia* implies an objective and lasting state rather than a subjective and fleeting feeling.

So the word "happiness" in modern English is ambiguous; it can mean either *eudaimonia* or *hēdonē*. And that is the difference—the three differences, really; all three of them almost always go together—between philosophers who follow Aristotle and those who follow Epicurus. Just about all subsequent ethical philosophers fit into these two categories. They are either ethical absolutists or relativists, spiritualists or materialists, and objectivists or subjectivists. Ethical absolutists say that happiness absolutely requires moral goodness, that this is universally true, always and everywhere, for everyone. Ethical spiritualists say that happiness is first of all and essentially in the soul and in the goods of the soul, rather than in the body and the satisfaction of bodily desires. Ethical objectivists say that happiness is first of all something you really are or have, not something you feel or think. Thus, you can be wrong about whether you are happy or not. It sounds strange to say that in modern English; that is why the old-fashioned English word "blessedness" is a clearer translation of Aristotle's *eudaimonia* than the word "happiness."

Actually, I must make one correction to the oversimplified classification above. Most hedonists, like Epicurus, concentrate on spiritual or mental pleasures more than bodily pleasures because they are under our control much more than bodily pleasures are. Most hedonists are semi-materialists rather than total materialists; that is, they see the role of the mind as necessary but instrumental: it is the servant or scout for the body and the senses. For rationally (spiritually) calculating which things will give us pleasure and which things will give us pain is also necessary if we are to attain pleasure.

Many hedonists, like Epicurus, take this semi-spiritualism a step further and say that pleasures of the mind or spirit are higher or better than pleasures of the body, even though they are not as intense. Wild parties, unbridled lust, and greed and pride, though they please us at the time, are not the most pleasant pleasures. In fact, they bring pain and regret. But hedonists still say that it is pleasure rather than moral justice or righteousness or duty that is the greatest good, and that since pleasure is subjective ("different strokes for different folks"), moral goodness is subjective.

The main problem with hedonism is its egotism. Pleasure is personal—i.e., individual and private. Why then should I be concerned about other people's pleasure? Almost everyone admires altruism and disapproves of egotism and selfishness—Satanists, Nietzsche, Sartre, and Ayn Rand are the only exceptions I can think of—but *why*? Why should I give up some of my own personal pleasures for other people's? Why should I work for the common good and not just for my own? What justifies self-sacrifice? And even if I don't have to *subtract* anything—i.e., sacrifice anything—why should I *add* concern with other people's good to my concern for my own?

One possible answer is that there is no answer. Just be an egotist and let others also be egotists. Perhaps radical individualism will produce maximum happiness for everyone. Perhaps working for others is being a busybody and a nuisance. That is essentially Ayn Rand's philosophy. But it is a hard one to believe when you are starving or drowning.

Another possible answer is that working for others makes us happier. We know that by experience. Selfishness is destructive to the self and its happiness. This is true, but the problem with that is it's still using others merely as a means to my own selfish ends. My heart still loves myself and my own happiness alone, but my head sees that I need to do good deeds to feel contented. I don't really love or care about others and their happiness as an end, only as a means to my own end of pleasure. The problem with this is that no one wants to be treated as a means. If you don't want others to treat you merely as a means to their pleasure, what justifies you in treating them as a mere means to your own pleasure? It violates the Golden Rule ("Do unto others what you want others to do to you"), which almost everyone recognizes as right.

So is the Golden Rule valid? If not, why does almost everyone think and feel that it is? If it is valid, what makes it valid? Why should I obey it instead of my own purely private desire for pleasure? Why isn't selfishness the logical consequence of hedonism? Why shouldn't I walk out of my promises, commitments, contracts, duties, and marriages if they bring me pain rather than pleasure? Why sacrifice my pleasure for yours? It seems that a hedonist can live a good life only if he or she violates his own philosophy. Shouldn't your philosophy of life and your life match rather than contradict?

Epicurus was at least consistent. He lived his philosophy. He built a beautiful garden and surrounded it with a wall and retreated into his garden whenever anyone or anything outside was unpleasant to him. He invited many people into his garden, especially prostitutes, but only those who gave him pleasure. He was careful never to associate with those whose poverty or problems would disturb his tranquility. Fortunately, he never married or had children.

Epicurus' hedonism was a natural fit with Protagoras' moral relativism, since pleasure (which is the only good for hedonism) is relative to subjective feelings. One can be a relativist without being a hedonist (if one defines the moral good as something other than pleasure), but one can hardly be a hedonist without being a relativist, since pleasure is relative.

SELECTED BIBLIOGRAPHY

William De Witt Hyde, *The Five Great Philosophies of Life*

14

Epictetus
(AD 55–135):
Stoicism

Stoicism was the single most popular ethical philosophy in the late Roman Empire. Its most famous book is the *Meditations* of Emperor Marcus Aurelius, the only successful philosopher-king in history. Its simplest and shortest work is the *Enchiridion* of Epictetus.

What we mean today by a "Stoic" or by being "stoical" is someone who keeps his emotions under the control of his reason, who endures pain and inconvenience without complaining, and who takes moral virtue very seriously. This is historically accurate, though oversimplified.

For Stoicism there are only three virtues that are essential:

1. the detachment from what cannot be changed (that's the negative half);
2. the will and courage to change what can be changed (that's the positive half); and
3. the wisdom to know the difference.

If you remember the image of the orders received by the fleet of ships in our Introduction, you can see that Stoicism concentrates almost exclusively on the second of the three ethical questions: individual virtues, or keeping the ship of your own soul shipshape. Stoicism does not claim to know the answer to ultimate questions like the existence, character, and purposes of God or life after death (which fall under the first of the three ethical questions), nor does it claim to have a program for social or political ethics (the third question). It is a way of keeping your individual moral sanity in a skeptical and confused world and your moral honor in a decadent world. In this way, it is like Epicureanism, since both retreat from the world—Epicurus into his garden and the Stoics into their souls. But in other ways, Stoicism and Epicureanism are opposites. Stoics are as unconcerned about pleasures as Epicureans are unconcerned about moral virtues, duties, and laws.

The fundamental argument for Stoicism is its personal "pay-off." It claims to solve the problem of pain and suffering better than anything else can. In that way it is like Buddhism, though unlike Buddhism it is not a religion or a mystical transformation of consciousness, only a rational philosophy. Buddha summarized his whole philosophy in the "four noble truths":

1. that all of life is full of suffering ("to live is to suffer");
2. that the cause of suffering is desire, which creates the gap between desire and satisfaction;
3. that the way to end suffering is to end desire; and
4. that the way to end desire is the "noble eightfold path" of desire-reduction and ego-reduction in each of life's eight basic areas, inner and outer, intellectual and emotional.

The simple essence of Stoicism is Buddha's "third noble truth": the way to end suffering is to end desire. Epictetus says, "Remember that desire demands the attainment of that which you desire . . . that he who fails of his desire is disappointed . . . [therefore] altogether restrain desire, for if you desire any of the things not within your own power, you must necessarily be disappointed. . . . Demand not that events should happen as you wish, but wish them to happen as they do happen."

As you can see in its list of three virtues above (paragraph 3), Stoicism divides life into two areas: what we can control and what we cannot (that is its "wisdom"). It wastes no energy or desire in trying (hopelessly) to change the unchangeable (that is its "detachment") but spends all its energy on the cultivation of personal virtue, which is the only area of life that is always under our control. The psychological principle here is that suffering is not simply a material event, like a knife cutting our flesh or a robber removing our wealth, but our negative evaluation of and reaction to that event. We desired pleasure or wealth; that is why we hate pain or poverty. We cannot change the external component of suffering, but we can change the internal one, our attitude. Epictetus says, "Men are disturbed not by things but by the view which they take of things." Suppose you lose your job, your spouse, your money, or even your life. What gives you pain is not these events in themselves but your attachment to these things that you lost. They are not good or bad in themselves, but your thoughts and desires make them good to you. (That sounds like Protagoras' relativism.) As Hamlet says, "There is nothing either good or bad, but thinking [or desiring] makes it so." We cannot change or control most of the things that come to us, but we can control and change our attitude toward them. So if we stop desiring these things, we will stop suffering when they are lost. It's as simple as that in theory, though of course it is not easy in practice to control our passions, desires, and fears.

But there is a "payoff," and it is what everyone wants: if not happiness, at least the peace that comes from the abolition of pain and unhappiness. Epictetus says, "If you take for your own only that which is your own [i.e., your attitudes] and view what belongs to others [i.e., everything else] just as it really is, then no one will ever compel you, no one will restrict you. . . . If you want to be a man of modesty and fidelity, who shall prevent you?"

This is a kind of rational Nirvana, for "Nirvana" means "extinction" and the point of both Buddhism and Stoicism is that if you "extinguish" your passions, you also "extinguish" your pain. If you want nothing but virtue, you can have everything you want. If you want the gifts of fortune (riches, fame, glory, honor, beauty, pleasure, power), you will have to sing the most famous line of the world's richest philosopher: "You can't always get what you want."

Epicureans taught that pleasure was the only good. Stoics taught that virtue was the only good. For Epicureans taught that we are essentially bodies (with minds attached), while Stoics taught that we are essentially souls (with bodies attached). If we wanted to be critical, we might say that for Epicureans we are animals and for Stoics we are angels. Or, to be satirical, we might call Epicureans dogs and Stoics cats, or Epicureans slobs and Stoics snobs.

The Stoics argued, against the Epicureans, that pleasure was only a byproduct of the true good, as the pleasant taste of a healthy food is a byproduct of the presence of the real food. The pleasure does not keep you healthy or alive; the food does. The Epicureans sought the byproduct instead of the product. The Stoics insisted that only virtuous people are happy because they seek not happiness but virtue.

The Stoics also argued, against the Epicureans, that if the good is identical to pleasure, then the bad must be identical to pain. But this does not account for the obvious fact that good people often suffer pain and evil people often experience pleasures.

The most essential and the most demanding of the three virtues of Stoicism is the virtue of cool, rational detachment and self-control, the control of the passions and desires and emotions by the reason. (But remember that "reason" in premodern thought does not mean merely "logical reasoning" but also and above all "wisdom, insight, understanding.") They argued that our feelings are unfree unless they are subject to our reason and our will (when our will is itself subject to reason), for reason (and will) is the only thing in us that is free. So to maximize freedom, Stoicism minimizes feelings.

There is obviously something appealing about Stoicism. Not only does it minimize pain and produce serenity (though at a price), but it takes moral virtue very seriously, especially its three virtues of wisdom, self-control, and detachment.

Yet it also seems to have something not only unappealing but appalling. For one thing, it tends to Pharisaical pride and self-righteousness rather than humility. For another thing, it demands the suppression of love and compassion. If you really want to avoid the deepest pains of heartbreak, you dare not give your heart to anyone. It ignores the deep psychological truth that the only whole heart is one that has been broken. Thus, Epictetus gives us some chillingly insensitive pieces of advice, such as: "When you see anyone weeping for grief . . . be ready to say 'what hurts this man is not this occurrence itself—for another man might not be hurt by it—but the view he chooses to take of it.' . . . Accommodate yourself to him and, if need be, groan with him, but take heed not to groan inwardly too." The Stoical detachment from one's own sufferings may be noble, but the detachment from others' seems cold and cruel. And if we may not sympathize with others' sorrows, we may not rejoice in others' joys either: "Be not elated by any excellence not your own."

Finally, Stoicism may save your sanity in a dying world, but it seems passive and pessimistic. Its emphasis on the acceptance of what we cannot change minimizes hope, effort, courage, risk-taking, and optimism. "Seek not to have things happen as you choose them, but rather choose that they should happen as they do"—could Epictetus preach that philosophy to a Jew in Auschwitz?

SELECTED BIBLIOGRAPHY

Epictetus, *Enchiridion*

Marcus Aurelius, *Meditations*

Three Medieval
Christian Saints

15

St. Augustine
(AD 354–430):
Love and the Heart

The contrast between Augustine and the Stoics is very sharp. For Augustine himself, personally, and for Augustine's philosophical psychology and ethics, the heart and its loves are not to be suppressed but perfected, for the heart is the central thing. Whether the "heart" is taken to mean the seat of the emotions or the will, the heart is what loves. And for Augustine, as for Solomon in the Proverbs, the fundamental ethical wisdom is to "keep thy heart with all diligence, for out of it are all the issues of life." Augustine wrote, "Pondus meum amor meus"—my love is my weight, my gravity, my destiny. I move where my loves move. A materialist (like Epicurus) says, "You are what you eat." All evil is pain, or disordered "stuff." A rationalist (like Plato) says, "You are what you think." All evil is ignorance, or disordered thought. A lover (like Augustine) says, "You are what you love." All evil is disordered love. Medieval statues of Augustine always show him with an open Bible in one hand and a burning heart in the other.

For Augustine, in the last analysis there are only two fundamental ethical options because there are only two fundamentally different loves, and thus two kinds of people. The basic theme of his classic *The City of God* is that two loves have made two (invisible) cities (communities): the love of God to the rejection of one's self (of egotism) has made the City of God; the love of self to the rejection of God has made the City of Man. These two opposite cities have two opposite destinies, heaven and hell. That is the fundamental theme of both world history, which Augustine describes in *The City of God*, and the drama of an individual life, which he describes in the *Confessions*.

The *Confessions* is much shorter, easier, and more dramatic than *The City of God*. In fact, it is one of the most popular Christian books ever written, next to the Bible. And its fundamental theme, the lesson of Augustine's life, is the most oft-quoted Christian sentence outside the Bible: "Thou [God] hast made us for thyself, and [therefore] our hearts are restless until they rest in thee." This is not just piety; it is reasoning and argument. The evidence, available to everyone, is the restlessness and dissatisfaction of the human heart. We all have a "lover's quarrel with the world." It is good, but it is not enough. On the one hand, our happiness is shallow and limited and transient; on the other hand, we want it to be deep and unlimited and forever. That is the double evidence. And Augustine offers the Christian story—the perfect God designing and creating man perfect and then man freely falling from that state into sin (alienation from God) and consequent misery—as the only adequate theoretical explanation of that double evidence, and Christ and the reconnection with God as the only adequate practical solution.

This is religion, of course, but it is also philosophy and rational argument. In fact, it is basic scientific method: testing the hypothesis or theory (Christianity) by its ability to explain the evidence (the universal human experience of the "restless heart," or "You can't always get what you want"). And it is ethics, for it offers God (through Christ) as the only adequate answer to the first and most important ethical question of the *summum bonum* or supreme good.

Along the way, in the *Confessions*, Augustine also addresses classic philosophical problems like how finite man can conceive an infinite God, how a good God can allow evil, fate and free will, the nature of time, and moral relativism. Augustine does not sharply separate faith and reason, religion and philosophy. He is an intensely practical philosopher: though he is an intellectual genius, he is not much concerned with method (which is only the road or the roadmap) but always with truth and joy, which is the home at the end of the road and how to actually get there. Augustine is a saint, but not a plaster saint. He has a heartbeat, and he spills his blood as well as his mind onto his pages.

SELECTED BIBLIOGRAPHY

Augustine, *Confessions* (Sheed translation)
Peter Kreeft, *I Burned for Your Peace*

16

St. Anselm
(AD 1033–1109):
That Than Which Nothing
Greater Can Be Thought

St. Anselm is famous for a single argument, which almost every ordinary person finds both brilliant and unconvincing. It is an argument for the existence of God that history has dubbed "the ontological argument." ("Ontological" means "about being.") More ink has been spilled about this argument than about any other argument in the history of philosophy. I include it here because it is also implicitly an ethical argument.

The argument goes as follows. (Anselm's actual words are less clear but make the same point.)

1. We first define the being we are claiming to prove—namely, God—as "that than which nothing greater can be conceived," or the greatest conceivable being. If God is infinite, if his perfections are all unlimited, we cannot define him positively, since definitions are limits; but we can define him negatively, clearly distinguishing him from all that he is not (all imperfect beings). Atheists as well as theists must accept this definition because if they do not, they cannot say which God it is that

they do not believe in. (You can see this if you apply it to Santa Claus, the Loch Ness Monster, or Zeus.)

2. If you say that this "greatest conceivable being" does not exist, you say that he lacks one conceivable perfection: objectively real existence independent of your mind. For it is greater and more perfect to exist independent of the human mind than to exist only in the mind as a fantasy or mere concept.

3. But to say that the being that, by definition, lacks no conceivable perfection lacks this one conceivable perfection is self-contradictory. And since whatever is self-contradictory must be false, atheism must be false. And if atheism is false, theism must be true. The argument claims to prove that God exists by demonstrating that the proposition "God does not exist" is self-contradictory.

Most people cannot logically refute the argument, yet they commonsensically suspect that there is something wrong with it because you can't prove that anything really *exists* just by examining its definition. You can prove that X does not *mean* Y, or you can prove that X exists by showing that Y exists and that Y could not exist unless X existed, but you cannot deduce *existence* from mere *meaning*; you can only deduce one meaning from another or one existence from another. (Another way of putting the point is to say, with Kant, that "existence is not a predicate," or a property, or a perfection.)

I strongly suspect that common sense is right here (though some brilliant philosophers disagree, including Descartes, Spinoza, Leibniz, Hegel, and Plantinga). But Anselm's argument is not merely a metaphysical argument for God's existence; it has an ethical dimension too. Anselm is trying to lead the reader to God as the *summum bonum* or greatest good, the ultimate end of human life.

Here is the connection between the metaphysical and the ethical dimensions of Anselm's argument. Even if Anselm's argument fails to prove God's existence, it succeeds in giving an excellent definition of God as the being whose very essence is existence—i.e., who exists necessarily, rather than contingently (by being dependent on another being). The definition is only a definition, so it cannot prove that God exists, but it succeeds in defining God (negatively) and distinguishing God from every other being as "the being than which nothing greater can be conceived." The same can be said of the greatest good: it must be that than which nothing greater can be conceived. And thus we can deduce other attributes of this "greatest good" even if our argument cannot prove its existence.

This is what Anselm does at the end of his short, brilliant, densely packed book *Proslogion*. Since a good greater than any which can be conceived is greater than a good that *can* be conceived, the greatest good is greater than can be conceived. It is, as G.E. Moore demonstrated at length in his *Ethics*, what he called "non-natural"—i.e., not having a definable nature. It is what Wittgenstein called "mystical."

By the way, Wittgenstein clearly stated that his masterpiece the *Tractatus* is really about ethics, even though it never mentions ethics, because it defines "what can be said" and "what cannot be said," and ethics lies in the second category. By "ethics" he meant the whole ethical dimension, but also, most especially, the supreme good. The Bible says something similar: "What no eye has seen, nor ear heard, nor the human heart [thought] conceived, what [good] God has prepared for those who love him" (1 Cor. 2:9). And this is the "bottom line," the final conclusion, of Anselm's book in its last three chapters (24–26).

Just as the supreme good must transcend all contingent goods, the supreme being must transcend all contingent beings. The argument for God as the one necessary being is also the argument for God as the one necessary good.

This is the "one thing necessary" (see Luke 10:42) in which there is every good. Just as the logical conclusion of the ontological argument is for the mind to believe in God as supremely *true*, the practical conclusion is for the will to choose and for the heart to love God as supremely *good*: "Why, therefore, do you wander through many things, little man, by seeking [as the *summum bonum*] the goods of your soul and your body? Love the one good, in which all goods are, and it suffices. For what do you love, what do you desire, my soul? It is there; whatever you love, whatever you desire, is there."

He then applies this specifically to all the goods we desire: beauty, strength, freedom, life, contentment, inebriation, music, pleasure, wisdom, friendship, peace, power, honor, riches, security.

And then he adds love, which multiplies the joy: "But if anyone else whom you love altogether as yourself were to have the same blessedness, your joy would be doubled, because you would rejoice no less for him than for yourself. . . . Therefore, in that complete charity of the innumerable blessed angels and men, where no one loves another less than oneself, everyone will rejoice no differently for each other than for oneself. If, therefore, the heart of man will hardly grasp the joy it has from its own good alone, how will it be capable of so many and so great joys?"

Just as God is the one and only absolutely necessary *being* (the point of the ontological argument at the beginning of the book: that God exists necessarily, that God's essence is existence), he is also the one and only absolutely necessary *good* (which is the book's final conclusion).

It is essentially the same point Augustine made when he said, "Those who have God alone have everything, and those who have everything else but not God have nothing, and those who have God plus everything else do not have anything more than those who have God alone."

SELECTED BIBLIOGRAPHY

Anselm, *Proslogion*

17

St. Thomas Aquinas
(AD 1225–1274):
The Marriage of Christian
and Aristotelian Ethics

THE ROLE OF FAITH AND REASON IN ETHICS

Aquinas is a very large philosopher, intellectually as well as physically. He was too fat and too sympathetic to animals to ride donkeys, as most of his fellow monks did, so he walked between Italy and Paris many times. Like Aristotle, he has something to say about nearly everything, and, like Aristotle, it is usually a commonsensical middle position between two extremes.

Ethics is part of philosophy, but it is also part of religion. Aquinas, more than anyone else, is famous for a synthesis of philosophy and religion, of reason and faith, which could fairly be called the central task of the medieval mind.

The issue of the relation between them is put in Plato's dialogue *Euthyphro*, where Socrates asks Euthyphro whether an act is good because the gods will it, or love it, or are pleased by it, or whether the gods love it because it is good. If we substitute "God" for "the gods," we have the same problem. If we say, with Euthyphro, that an act is good only because God wills it, we are saying that faith, not reason, is the highest standard, since faith rather than reason knows (or claims to know) the will of God. Thus, faith must judge reason, not be judged by it. So faith can be irrational. That is one-half of the dilemma. But if we say, with Socrates, that God wills certain acts (of justice, charity, courage, etc.) because they are good, we are implicitly saying that reason is the highest standard, since reason knows, or claims to know, what is good. Thus, reason must judge faith, not be judged by it. So reason can be irreligious. That is the other half of the dilemma.

There are five possible answers to this dilemma.

1. Euthyphro's answer is faith without reason, religion without philosophy; thus, in ethics, a thing is good only because God (or gods) wills it. Many Muslim thinkers (but not all) hold this, following the ninth-century Ash'arites. Some Christian thinkers hold this (Tatian, Tertullian, Ockham, Luther) but not most. It is part of what is usually called "fundamentalism." An obvious problem with Euthyphro's answer ("the divine command theory") is that it makes God arbitrary. If God commanded you to hate everyone and forbade you to love anyone, hate would become good and love would become evil.

2. Socrates' answer seems to be reason without faith, philosophy without religion, or at least religion subordinated to reason. This seems unorthodox for religious Jews, Christians, and Muslims, who believe their faith is a divine revelation from God himself. In making faith subordinate to reason, it seems to make God subordinate to man, if the revelation that is the object of faith is from God's mind and reason is from man's mind. This answer makes it seem as if God has to keep checking whether he is a good God by looking at the Ten Commandments.

3. A third answer is (a) to affirm the validity of both faith, properly understood, and reason, properly used; (b) to affirm that both "go all the way up"; and (c) to say that they

never contradict each other because both ultimately come from God, like two books from the same author, who never contradicts himself. For God is the author of both human reason, which he designed as part of "the image of God" in man, and faith—i.e., *the* faith, which he revealed. This is the mainline answer of medieval thinkers, especially Augustine and Aquinas.

4. A fourth possible answer is that of thinkers who deny that either religious faith or philosophical reason can know the true good. Such thinkers include the ancient Sophists and modern atheists like Machiavelli, Hume, Mill, Nietzsche, and Sartre.

5. A fifth possible answer is simply to separate the two completely and say they are incompatible; to make two separate worlds out of them. This is an easy and convenient way of avoiding the dilemma, but it is unlivable and schizoid. If we are one person, not two, we must live in one reality, not two.

This question is about the epistemological *foundation* of ethics. Aquinas says that *both* natural human reason (and its power of moral conscience, which is an act of reason intuiting good and evil) *and* faith in divine revelation are valid foundations for ethics and that the two partially overlap, so that there are three kinds of moral truths: (1) there are many things in philosophical (rational) ethics that are not part of religious faith (e.g., the morality or immorality of capitalism), (2) there are many things in religious ethics that are not philosophically knowable by reason (e.g., God's choice to love us), and (3) there are many things that are part of both (e.g., the Golden Rule).

Aquinas also argues that there are not, and cannot be, any contradictions between the two—between faith and reason in general or between the ethics known by faith and the ethics known by reason. And he gives two reasons for this: (1) because truth cannot contradict truth, and (2) because God is the author of both the revealed religion and its morality *and* the human mind's innate power to know truth, including moral truth. He is the author of both of those ethical "books," and he does not ever contradict himself.

That question was about the epistemological basis for ethics. (The basis, for Aquinas, is both faith and reason.) An important consequence for ethics is Aquinas' definition of moral law as an ordinance not of will first of all but of reason, both for God and for man.

FOUR KINDS OF LAW

Aquinas' definition of a "law" has five parts. A law is (1) an ordinance (or command) (2) of (based on) reason (3) for the common good (4) made by the (divine or human) ruler of a community (5) and promulgated (to that community).

There are four kinds of law. Two are supernatural and two are natural, and two are for all times and places while two are not.

1. *Eternal law* is the law in God's eternal mind and will for the life of the whole creation, including the human community. It is goodness itself.
2. *Natural law* is the creature's participation in the eternal law. Subrational creatures do this by their subrational and unfree behavior—thus the laws of physics and of animal instinct. Man, unlike all other known creatures in the universe, is not merely *under* the eternal law but actively participates in it by knowing it by reason (conscience) and obeying or disobeying it by a free choice of the will. All men know the primary precepts of the natural (moral) law; they are things we just "can't not know."
3. *Divine law* is law that God makes for one people or time but not another—e.g., the civil and liturgical laws for ancient Israel, or God's call to a prophet.

4. *Human law* is made (or "posited," thus the modern term for this is "positive law") by human beings (congresses, kings, CEOs, etc.). They have a human origin and an only-human validity; so since man, unlike God, is fallible, there can be bad human laws. (But this judgment assumes that there is at least one higher kind of law that is the standard for that judgment.)

We have a moral obligation to obey all human laws that are not bad ones for the sake of the common good. We also have an obligation to disobey bad human laws that contradict any one of the three kinds of higher law and to try to change bad laws into good ones. Thus, it is only the belief in some higher law than human law that justifies protest, rebellion, and sometimes even tyrannicide. Without such a belief one must either be a stick-in-the-mud conservative or a rebel whose only justification is might, not right.

Note that (1) and (3) are supernatural, but (2) and (4) are not, and that (1) and (2) are unchangeable, but (3) and (4) are not. Eternal law is supernatural and unchangeable; natural law is natural and unchangeable; divine law is supernatural and changeable; and human law is natural and changeable.

WHAT IS A GOOD PERSON? THE VIRTUES

Aquinas' answer to this question is not original, but part of the common tradition from Plato and the Bible onward. The seven foundational virtues are wisdom, courage, moderation, justice, faith, hope, and charity.

Virtues are good habits; vices are bad habits. The total package of virtues and vices make up a person's moral character. Wisdom, courage, moderation, and justice are the "four cardinal virtues" on the natural level. And faith, hope, and charity are the three "theological virtues"; because both their object and their origin is God, they are the supernatural virtues.

Wisdom, or prudence, is the moral virtue that is also an intellectual virtue, a good habit of thought. It is the habit of judging rightly about good and evil human acts. Without it, no virtue is rational; without light, nothing is seen.

Courage, or fortitude, is necessary to practice any virtue. It fights against all obstacles to the good despite personal sufferings.

Moderation, or temperance, or self-control, is the virtue that most clearly distinguishes civilization from barbarism. It consists in subjecting the passions to reason and not allowing any one passion to rage without limit. Like Aristotle, Aquinas rejects both Stoicism, which views passions as intrinsically bad, and Epicureanism, which views them as intrinsically good. They are raw material to be formed by wise reason and courageous will.

Justice is to do what is right, or fair, and gives each person and each power in oneself what is due to him, her, or it.

Faith, hope, and charity are the three powers of the soul responding to God. Faith is the mind's adherence, through belief, to all the truths God has revealed on the reasonable grounds that God can neither be deceived nor deceive. Hope is the desires' adherence to God's promises. It is faith directed to the future. Charity is the will's adherence to God's will, which is love: "You shall love the Lord your God with all your heart . . . [and] your neighbor as yourself" (Mark 12:30–31). (Love is essentially an act of will, not a feeling; that is why it can be commanded.)

Each of these virtues has an obvious opposite vice. The opposite of wisdom is folly, which is theoretical but also practical error. The opposite of courage is cowardice (but also foolhardiness). The opposite of temperance is intemperance (addiction to anger, lust, or greed). The opposite of justice is injustice. (Mercy is not unjust but presupposes justice in going beyond it.) The opposite of faith is deliberate unbelief. The opposite of hope is despair, and also presumption. The opposite of love is hate, but the most common opposite of love is indifference ("sloth").

These are not the only virtues and vices or even the only essential ones. Honesty, for example, is an essential natural virtue, and dishonesty (especially with oneself) an intolerable vice; and humility (before God) is an essential supernatural virtue, and pride (arrogance) an intolerable vice. But these seven are the essential virtues that perfect the three essential human powers that distinguish us from animals: the intellect, the will, and the passions.

EIGHT CANDIDATES FOR THE GREATEST GOOD

Ethics is most fundamentally about good and evil. Evil is relative to good (as its opposite, its enemy, its deprivation), not vice versa. So the greatest question in ethics is the question of what is the greatest good.

Philosophers, like ordinary, sane people, have come up with pretty much the same alternative answers to that question in all times, places, and cultures.

Aquinas' summary of eight of those answers, while not complete (he does not include political activity or human love and friendship as separate answers), considers most of the most popular of these answers in order. (His order is from the worst answer to the best.) They are wealth, honor, fame or glory, power, bodily goods (health), pleasure, goods of the soul (wisdom and virtue), and God.

Aquinas first establishes that Aristotle is right to call our supreme end "happiness" (*eudaimonia*—i.e., blessedness, not mere contentment). He then asks which of these goods gives us happiness. (They are all *goods*, but there can be only one greatest good.)

1. Wealth (money) is only a means (a "means of exchange"), not an end; and the things money can buy are also means to our happiness, not happiness itself.

2. Honor is external to us; it is in the one honoring. And it is given to us only because of some other good for which we are honored.

3. Human fame or glory is similar. It consists in other people's knowledge of us, and this is the effect, not the cause, of our good. It is not, like God's knowledge, creative of its object.

4. Power is a means, not an end; it can be used for good or evil; and it is corruptible. (The same could be said about "freedom," which is similar to power.)

5. Bodily goods (primarily health) do not raise us above animals. In fact, some animal surpasses us in every bodily good. But no animal surpasses us in happiness (or in unhappiness).

6. Pleasure is indeed sought as an end, but it comes only as an effect of the presence of some good that pleases us. It does not answer the question of the identity of that good.

7. Goods of the soul (wisdom and virtue) are higher, but they are still only like a road rather than a destination, since the soul, like the body, is in time and always growing toward an end. It can no more be its own end than a runner can be his own goal line or an arrow its own target.

8. In the end, no finite, temporal, created good can satisfy our thirst for perfect happiness. We seek the universal good, which transcends all partial and particular goods. And this is nowhere in this world; it is either nowhere or in the perfect good, which is a description of God alone.

But if "no natural desire is in vain," if we do not have natural desires for nonexistent objects, and if we have a natural desire for the perfect good, for perfect happiness, then this good must exist.

So parallel to Aquinas' famous arguments for God as first cause (the argument that nothing less suffices to account for the existence of the universe), he gives us an argument for God as our last end, and it is the same argument: that nothing less suffices. "Our hearts are restless until they rest in thee."

There is much more detail and many more issues in Aquinas' ethics, but these are four of the most basic ones.

SELECTED BIBLIOGRAPHY

Peter Kreeft, *A Shorter Summa*
Peter Kreeft, ed., *Summa of the Summa*
Peter Kreeft, *Practical Theology* (anthology)
G.K. Chesterton, *St. Thomas Aquinas: "The Dumb Ox"*
Étienne Gilson, *Moral Values and the Moral Life*

An Interlude about
Modern vs. Medieval Ethics

Between Aquinas in the thirteenth century and Kant late in the eighteenth century, there are no really major new philosophers in the field of ethics. Most of the "big ideas" we can learn from thinkers in these centuries (like Machiavelli, Hobbes, and Hume) are negative ideas, ideas that reduce rather than expand the meaning and importance of ethics, at least as ethics has been traditionally and commonsensically conceived by almost all previous philosophers and sages except the Sophists.

The most obvious reason for this decline in ethics is the decline of religion. Religion has always been, throughout history, the strongest basis and reinforcement for ethics. It is not true that all our knowledge of ethics, or our belief in ethics, or our taking ethics seriously, depends on our knowledge of religion, or our belief in religion, or even on our taking religion seriously. (Remember the argument between Socrates and Euthyphro.) But it is true that every religion contains an ethical dimension as part of its very essence, and for almost all premodern societies and individuals, religion was the strongest psychological force in giving moral meaning, purpose, and value to human life.

A second factor in the decline of ethics is that politics becomes much more important in modern philosophy as both ethics and religion become less important. The most obvious reason for this is that we need some absolute to judge relative things, some center from which to judge peripheral things, and with the decline of religion and ethics, politics tends to take their place.

The old politics was simply social ethics; there was no double standard for individual and social justice in Plato, Aristotle, Augustine, or Aquinas. But the new politics, beginning with Machiavelli, is "the politics of the possible," not of the ideal. Insofar as the question of the *summum bonum* comes up at all, it is answered by typically modern philosophers in a radically new way; insofar as it is considered at all, it is assumed to be not the conformity of the soul to objective reality (which was conceived as containing a moral dimension) by means of moral virtue and wisdom, but the conformity of objective reality to the wishes of the soul as implemented by our technology, "man's conquest of nature" (Francis Bacon). This new notion of objective reality was considered as not having a moral dimension but as mere matter to be known by science and manipulated by technology.

In the modern period, Edmund Burke and Alexis de Tocqueville are pretty much the only major political philosophers who apply ethical categories to politics not merely as a kind of postscript ("Don't forget your umbrella when you go out") but essentially.

Unlike premodern politics, modern politics is bipolar: left versus right, or "liberal" versus "conservative." But I have never understood what is "liberal" about communism or what is "conservative" about Nazism or fascism. In fact, the terms "liberal" and "conservative" have almost opposite meanings when you cross the Atlantic, for both classical American "conservatism" and classical European "liberalism" center on individual rights and liberties and opposition to political totalitarianism.

A third, related reason that is often given for the decline of ethics in early modern philosophy is the rise of science, due mainly to the rise of the scientific method. You naturally "go with your best pitch," and modernity is vastly superior to all premodern cultures in science. Thus, the main focus of modern philosophy, beginning with Descartes, is not metaphysics, ethics, or philosophical theology but epistemology and its close cousin methodology. Descartes, who is usually regarded as the father of modern philosophy, began the experiment of doing philosophy by the scientific method. He never got around to applying that method to ethics, however. We might regard Kant as his successor in this neglected enterprise, two centuries later; for Kant's ethics, while not scientific in the sense of being empirical, is scientific in the sense of being almost mathematically logical and clear.

Three Modern
Political Philosophers

18

Niccolò Machiavelli (AD 1469–1527): The Separation between Ethics and Politics

Machiavelli effectively put an end to the application of ethics to politics. Not all of his successors agree with him; in fact, all of them try to modify his scandalous radicalism in some way. Yet almost all of them, to some degree, agree with the essential Machiavellian revolution. Politics is now "the art of the possible," not the ideal.

Machiavelli is not only "the founder of modern political philosophy" (according to Leo Strauss) but also the most famous example of the assumption that ethics is not about objective reality but about mere "ideals" or "values"—i.e., the assumption that ethics (which is about what is good) is not based on metaphysics (which is about what is real). In other words, the modern assumption is that Plato is wrong about his most fundamental assertion, that the ultimate *reality* is "the Good." If Plato is wrong about that, then we have to choose between ethical "ideals" and the "real world"; we have to choose between ethics and "realpolitik," which means asking first of all what works rather than what is morally good.

There are various ways to summarize this Machiavellian point. One is that "the end justifies the means." Machiavelli did not write those words, but they reflect his main point: that there are no absolute or ultimate ends or goods but only instrumental, practical, utilitarian goods; that Plato and all the premodern ethical philosophers (except the Sophists) were merely dreaming when they spoke of "the Good" or "Justice" as a thing in itself. Justice is whatever those in power say it is; therefore power, not justice, is the absolute in human life. Justice, or goodness, may be the absolute *ideal* for "dreamy" philosophers like Plato, but it is not the absolute *reality*.

This is an implicit metaphysics: that objective reality does not include an ethical dimension; that the only real world is the visible world inside Plato's "cave," not the invisible world outside it. Obviously, this implies atheism, though Machiavelli could not afford to be honest enough to admit that, since he lived in a time when atheists were not tolerated. But ordinary people knew it and called Machiavelli "the devil's son." The English name for the devil, "Old Nick," comes from Machiavelli's first name, Niccolò. Machiavelli divides all the forces in human life into two, which he calls *virtu* (strength, power, effectiveness, all the things that are under your control) and *fortuna* (chance, luck, all the things not under your control); and his formula for success is the conquest of *fortuna* by *virtu*, or at least the maximization of *virtu* and the minimization of *fortuna*. The formula reduces life to a science.

And since other people are part of your *fortuna*, it is important to put them under the category of your *virtu* to control them. This is done by fear and force, not love and trust; for "it is much safer to be feared than loved, for men will fear you when *you* will, but they will love you when *they* will." Another corollary of the same principle about *virtu* and *fortuna* is that "armed prophets succeed, unarmed prophets fail."

The refutation of this apparently very logical philosophy is simply the empirical facts of life and history. Individual lives and political regimes based on fear have proved fragile; tyrants and "armed prophets" always fail, while it is the "unarmed prophets" like Socrates, Jesus, and Buddha whose lives are happy and whose regimes last. Machiavelli's principles simply do not explain the empirical facts. It is him whom the facts of history and life have proved to be the starry-eyed idealist and ideologist, and it is the traditional moralist whom the facts have proved to be the commonsense realist and the successful entrepreneur at the business of life, in the long run.

SELECTED BIBLIOGRAPHY

Niccolò Machiavelli, *The Prince*
Peter Kreeft, *Socrates Meets Machiavelli*

19

Thomas Hobbes
(AD 1588–1679):
Power as the Good

The key to Hobbes' philosophy is very simple: everything real is material. Hobbes is a consistent materialist, and he applies this principle to every division of philosophy: metaphysics, theology, cosmology, anthropology, epistemology, language, ethics, and politics.

Thought, concepts, mind, ideas, thinking, knowing, persons, souls, spirits, angels, God, gods, good and evil, right and wrong, virtue and vice—these terms, according to Hobbes, either are meaningless or have a strictly material meaning. For instance, Hobbes says that he is not an atheist and that he believes God exists but is made of matter. Thinking also exists but is simply picturing; a concept is a material copy of a material thing. Thus, there are no abstract ideas, no universal ideas. Man is nothing but body, mind is nothing but brain, truth is nothing but picturing, and goodness is nothing but the power to get what satisfies our desires.

Desires are the opposites of fears, and since our strongest desire is for pleasure, our strongest fear is pain, especially violent death. Since we are only animals (animals that can reason), and since we have no spiritual souls but only material bodies (that is

Hobbes' essential anthropology), and since matter is essentially competitive (two chunks of matter cannot occupy the same space at the same time), life is essentially a "king of the hill" contest, a zero-sum game. Thus, the "state of nature," the natural state of man, is a state of war and competition, a war of each against each and of each against all, a state in which life is nasty, solitary, poor, brutish, and short.

Most philosophers of the past (e.g., Plato, Aristotle, Augustine, Aquinas) noted that spiritual goods like knowledge, love, and beauty do not follow the law of matter. They multiply when shared, while material things diminish when shared. If I give you half of my wealth, power, land, or food, I have only half left. But if I give you some of my wisdom, love, or appreciation of beauty, I do not lose any; in fact, I may even gain more. (For example, we learn to understand, love, and appreciate things more by teaching others about them.) But Hobbes' materialism makes it impossible for him to admit this.

For Hobbes, we are all nothing but selfish by nature (as all matter is). Apparent examples of charity and goodwill are explained as disguises for selfish craving for pleasant feelings—e.g., he says that the cause of laughter is our sense of superiority to others; laughing is really sneering.

We are by nature nothing but selfish and wicked, but we can be compelled to act unselfishly and cooperatively and virtuously—that is, contrary to our nature—out of fear. So all the traditional moral virtues are unnatural matters of compulsion and motivated by fear. It is not conscience, virtue, or morality but effective totalitarian politics that is our only salvation.

Our only mitigation of this terrible "state of nature" is reason's invention of a "social contract" by which we give up all our rights to an absolute monarch in return for his protection. Hobbes defends totalitarian government as the only alternative to the civil war and violent death that are inevitable in the "state of nature." He called this absolute monarchy the "Leviathan," the Great Monster.

This has been the argument of every tyrant in history: give me your freedom and I will protect you. And it has proved very popular and successful. Like Machiavelli, Hobbes has for his "immoralism" (1) a strong inductive argument from history, as well as (2) a strong deductive argument from his materialist premise.

And as with Machiavelli, the strongest argument against him is from experience: both (1) the political experience of systems of democracy that appeal to free choice (which, by the way, Hobbes, consistent with his materialism, denies exist), and (2) the individual experience of self-consciousness, including the moral self-consciousness that we call "conscience," of an inner life, of an "I" that is not simply an "it," a subject of thinking and choosing that is not simply an object, a projecting machine that is not simply one of many images projected on the movie screen.

I might have chosen Karl Marx rather than Thomas Hobbes as a representative of materialism. I did not do so, even though Marx is much more famous, for two reasons. First, Hobbes has a complete philosophical system, which is internally consistent; Marx does not. Marx is a pragmatist and an ideologue. Second, Marxism has been massively tried and found wanting, both in theory (nearly every prediction Marx made has been disproved by history) and in practice (Marxism has been responsible for more murders of innocent ideological enemies than any other philosophy in history).

20

Jean-Jacques Rousseau (AD 1712–1778): Feeling as the Good

Four points:

1. Rousseau is in many ways the anti-Hobbes. If Hobbes is robotics, Rousseau is Woodstock.
2. Yet in the end he is as totalitarian as Hobbes.
3. But his is not a "hard totalitarianism" of power but a "soft totalitarianism" of feeling, and even of freedom (for he identifies freedom as a feeling).
4. This Romantic emotionalism and irrationalism is the natural swing of the pendulum or the seesaw against the opposite extreme of rationalism that was typical in his eighteenth-century "Enlightenment" culture.

He is the anti-Hobbes for a number of reasons:

a. For one thing, he is not a materialist. He exalts man's inner life and conscience, though he identifies it with feeling.
b. In fact, he claims to be religious, though he also identifies religiosity with feeling.

c. He claims to be a moralist, exalting "truth and virtue," though he reduces both to feelings.

d. He is an optimist about human nature, not a pessimist like Hobbes. He says that "the state of nature" is one of bliss and natural goodness, because (you guessed it!) everyone simply follows their feelings.

e. Evil comes not from human nature but from society, government, the invention of property, and (again, you guessed it) reliance on calculation rather than feeling.

f. In politics, Rousseau exalts freedom rather than authority or force. His philosophy was the guiding force behind the French Revolution.

Yet the ideal society for this anti-Hobbes is just as totalitarian as Hobbes' absolute monarchy, in fact more so. It is an example of what Alexis de Tocqueville called "soft totalitarianism" rather than "hard totalitarianism," a sort of *Brave New World* rather than a *1984*. For in this supposedly ideal society of his, there is a single absolute and infallible authority over all of life, a kind of immanent God. Rousseau calls it "the general will," and it is a sort of spontaneous, collective "we-consciousness." It is not reason but will, the will of the society as a whole, and it is determined not by reason or religious revelation or by vote but by—surprise again—feeling and intuition. No other authorities are allowed. Nothing is private, everything is public. This is the exact and essential formula for totalitarianism.

As Tocqueville pointed out in his classic book praising both democracy and America—entitled *Democracy in America*—there are two forms of totalitarianism, not just one. "Hard" totalitarianism uses power. Its authority is the will of the prince, or the king, or the dictator. "Soft" totalitarianism uses free choice, not individually but collectively. Its authority is consensus, or agreement. It is free and democratic totalitarianism. Totalitarianism and freedom are not incompatible, and neither are totalitarianism

and democracy. For these three terms are answers to three different questions. Totalitarianism is an answer to the question: How
much power does the public social, civil, state authority have? And
the answer is total power, power over all of human life. Freedom
is an answer to the different question: What human spiritual or
psychological power creates and maintains this public authority?
And Rousseau's answer is: free will, choice, the will of the people.
Thus, *vox populi, vox dei*—"the voice of the people is the voice
of God." In Rousseau, this is determined by (surprise, surprise!)
feeling. Finally, democracy is an answer to a third question, the
question of who holds the power. And its answer is: the *demos*,
the masses, the people at large—i.e., by everyone equally. Totalitarianism is quite compatible with both freedom and democracy,
as we can see in Rousseau.

Rousseau is often regarded as the father of Romanticism,
a movement in culture, literature, music, and philosophy that
glorified feeling and emotion and minimized reason. This was
a reaction to the glorification by the so-called "Enlightenment"
of scientific reason as the solution to all human problems. The
reaction was inevitable because the meaning of "reason" had
shrunk radically. When Aristotle defined man as "the rational
animal," he meant by "reason" all that distinguishes man from
the beasts, including intellectual intuition, moral conscience,
aesthetic appreciation and creativity, and religious belief, not
just logical calculation. Even Aristotle's logic, as distinct from
modern "symbolic logic," began not with propositions, which
were either simply true or simply false, but with terms, which had
to be understood by an act of intellectual intuition, not a process
of calculative reasoning. These terms had to be understood and
defined before we could rightly calculate how they were related
as subjects and predicates in propositions.

In Rousseau's time, science had proved so spectacularly
successful that all other dimensions of reason had been forgotten
or denigrated. When Pascal famously wrote that "the heart has its

reasons that the reason does not know," he was presupposing the ancient, broad meaning of "reason" in speaking of the "reasons" of the heart. For Pascal, as in ancient and medieval philosophy, "reason" was not reduced to scientific calculation, and "heart" was not reduced to feeling and emotion. Once the rich, broad term "reason" had been narrowed to mere calculation, the rich biblical term "heart" also was narrowed to mere feeling, and the two extremes were opposed to each other like two children on opposite sides of a seesaw.

But even in the realm of feelings, we can see an essential distinction between (1) the nonrational feelings we share with the other animals, such as contentment and discontent, pleasure and pain, fearfulness and boldness, and (2) the specifically human feelings, the "rational" feelings, such as compassion, generosity, hope, trust, courage, appreciation of beauty, and many forms of love, as well as their negative opposites: cold-heartedness, stinginess, despair, mistrust, cowardice, insensitivity, and many forms of lovelessness. All these specifically human feelings of the human "heart" used to be classified as part of "reason" in the broader sense, for two reasons: first, irrational, sub-human animals could not experience them; and second, we naturally hold ourselves and each other responsible for these good and bad "rational" feelings, thus implying that we have at least some freedom and power to affirm or deny them, but we have neither power over nor responsibility for the "irrational," merely animal feelings that are dependent wholly on the autonomic nervous system.

Rousseau's idolization of feeling is destructive, but it is a natural reaction to hard, narrow rationalism. A human without a heart is as inhuman as one without a head.

Three Classic
Modern Ethical Alternatives

21

David Hume
(AD 1711–1776):
Emotivist Ethics

Hume and Rousseau are opposites in many ways:

1. Hume is an "Enlightenment" rationalist, while Rousseau is an antirationalist.

2. Hume is a materialist and almost certainly an atheist (though he never admitted this in print), while Rousseau is (or claims to be) "spiritual" and "religious"—though the sincerity of this claim is rendered questionable by the fact of his four faked conversions to get money out of rich and gullible old ladies, and by the fact that he disposed of all five of his illegitimate children in orphanages which had, he knew, an 80 percent death rate, and refused to even give them names, despite the pleas of his mistress.

3. Hume's method of philosophizing is objective, empirical, and scientific, while Rousseau's is subjective, intuitive, and personal.

4. Hume's essential interests are epistemology and science, while Rousseau's are ethics and politics. For Hume, ethics is a kind of postscript to his main work, while for Rousseau, ethics is at the heart of his philosophy.

5. When they met, their relationship was one of the most radical mutual misunderstandings in the history of philosophy. Hume invited Rousseau to England because he naïvely believed Rousseau's (wholly invented) complaints that he was being persecuted in France and offered him protection and help, connecting him with influential friends. Rousseau's paranoid reaction was to accuse Hume of plots to destroy him. It was like fire meeting water.

Yet despite these differences, what Rousseau and Hume have to say about ethics is essentially the same thing: that it is not a matter of reason or objective truth but a matter of feeling and subjective desire.

And this is the single most popular ethical philosophy in modern Western culture. In fact, it is probably this idea, more than any other, that most radically distinguishes our culture from all others in the history of the world. So we do well to explore Hume's argument for it carefully.

For Rousseau, this "big idea" (that moral values are subjective feelings) is put forth either as simply a feeling or as an intuitively self-evident truth, whereas for Hume it is the logical conclusion of a deductive argument. It is useful, therefore, to see from what premises Hume deduces this conclusion. For the laws of logic dictate that if the terms are not ambiguous, one of two things must be true about Hume's essential ethical argument: either (1) the premises are true and the logic is valid, and therefore the conclusion is true (that moral values are in fact only subjective feelings); or (2) the conclusion is false, and therefore there must be either a false premise or a logical mistake in the argument.

Hume is very intelligent, and his logic seems very tight, and therefore those who disagree with Hume's conclusion see his argument as a *reductio ad absurdum*, a reduction of his premise to absurdity by the absurd conclusion that follows from it; a demonstration that if you adopt all his premises you must logically believe his conclusion, which is ethically absurd. (For if ethics is only feelings, how can there be ethics at all? How can there be justice, or duty, or conscience, or obligation, or moral law, or right and wrong?)

Hume's premises are epistemological:

1. He begins by identifying everything we are aware of as either (a) "impressions" or (b) "ideas." "Impressions" include external and internal sensations.
2. He distinguishes impressions and ideas by their degree of "vividness": impressions are concrete and vivid while ideas are abstract and vague.
3. The causal relationship between them is that all ideas are copies of sense impressions and caused by them.
4. The propositions or declarative sentences (truth claims) that we make from these two sources are thus either (a) "relations of ideas" or (b) "matters of fact." Relations of ideas (like "2+2=4" or "X does not equal non-X" or "Unmarried men are men") are known by pure thought and provable by pure logic, by the law of noncontradiction alone, without any experience or knowledge of the real world. To deny them involves logical self-contradiction. Thus, they are certain. Matters of fact (like "The sky is blue" or "Birds lay eggs" or "Caesar crossed the Rubicon") are known only by sense observation. Their opposites are not self-contradictory; thus, they are never certain, only probable.

Now comes the application of this epistemology to ethics.

Moral statements such as "Murder is wrong" fit into neither of these two categories. Therefore, they are not statements of reason at all but of feeling. "That act of murder is bad" and "You are a bad person to have murdered another person" can mean only "I feel bad when I see you committing a murder." Moral judgments are projections of personal feelings onto acts and persons. They are like the color of our sunglasses, not of the real world.

Thus, all morality is "judgmentalism." The only moral mistake is to think there are such things as true or false moral judgments. Hamlet famously said, like the Sophists, that "there is nothing either good or bad, but thinking makes it so." Hume's only change is to substitute "feeling" for "thinking."

Of the three logically possible criticisms of any argument—ambiguous terms, logical fallacy, or false premises—the last seems the most likely regarding Hume's argument for ethics being only feelings. Why? Because there are other conclusions that Hume logically deduces from the same premises, conclusions which nearly everyone judges as false, in fact absurd—namely, that we have no rational grounds at all for believing in any of the following things: (1) God, (2) the soul, (3) life after death, (4) knowledge of universals like "All men are mortal," (5) knowledge of the future, (6) real causal relationships ("causality" is not visible), and (7) substances (beings, things, entities that possess visible attributes or cause visible events), including that entity that we call the self. (For Hume there is no substantial self, no "I," only successions of acts of thinking, sensing, and desiring.) Thus, religion, metaphysics, ethics, aesthetics, politics, psychology, and even physical science (which depends on the principle of causality) are removed from the realm of reason and objective truth by Hume's epistemological premises, for the same reasons objective moral values are. Hume is perhaps the most radical skeptic in the history of philosophy.

SELECTED BIBLIOGRAPHY

Peter Kreeft, *Socrates Meets Hume*
David Hume, *An Enquiry Concerning Human Understanding*

22

Immanuel Kant (AD 1724–1804): A Non-Metaphysical Moral Absolutism

For everyone, whether they are philosophers or not, there are two essential ethical options.

One view, which is the majority view in premodern cultures, is that there is an objective order of moral values, goods, ends, virtues, duties, etc., and we are good if and only if we obey them, conform to them. Our freedom, our choice, our power, our pleasure, our peace, our satisfaction, and our happiness are not the greatest good; they must be curbed by and conform to the already existing objective moral order of goods, or moral law, which is unchangeable in its essence and is not made by us or alterable by us any more than the truths of the multiplication table or the laws of physics are. Thus, morality is absolute, at least in its essential principles (or, for Kant, perhaps only its one essential principle), though not, of course, in its many changing applications. We could call this "objective morality."

The other view, which is more typically modern, is that we ourselves are the greatest good; our goodness, freedom, power, pleasure, peace, satisfaction, or happiness is the absolute and is not to be conformed to or limited by anything greater because there *is* nothing greater. Thus, morality is relative to us, to our reason or beliefs or will or feelings or desires. We could call this "subjective morality."

One of the many reasons why Kant is the single most important ethical philosopher of modern times is that he combined these two options by offering a morality whose essential definition of the good is duty rather than pleasure and thus is a kind of objective moral absolutism, but one which also identifies the good as personal freedom and autonomy, which is typically modern, rather than as conformity and obedience to any metaphysical order or objective truth, which Kant, for epistemological reasons, believed we could not know. In fact, Kant is in a way even more skeptical than Hume in his epistemology, for Hume at least believed we could know objective reality, or "things in themselves" as Hume called them, with probability, though not with certainty, while Kant believed we could not know them at all.

His most influential moral work is titled *Grounding for the Metaphysics of Morals*. This is a misleading title for two reasons.

First, he does not ground his moral philosophy in metaphysics, anthropology, psychology, or religion, but presents a moral philosophy that is self-grounded, in that it attempts to show that morality is logically self-evident—that all moral evil is irrational, in fact logically self-contradictory. For Kant, the essential law of morality is like the essential law of logic, the law of noncontradiction. (This will become evident in his first formulation of what he calls "the categorical imperative," below.)

Second, it is not a metaphysical system at all in the traditional sense of metaphysics—i.e., a philosophy of being; for the basic point of Kant's epistemology, which he calls his "Copernican Revolution in philosophy" and which he summarizes in his *Critique of Pure Reason* (probably the single most important book of philosophy in the last seven hundred years), is that traditional, objective metaphysics is impossible because we cannot know "things in themselves," only things as they appear to our actively structuring consciousness. We cannot x-ray appearances to find objective reality behind or within them, because all meaning, form, order, or structure comes not *to* us from objective reality but *from* us, from our consciousness. This occurs on what we would today call an unconscious level, but in a way that is both universal (the same for all men) and necessary (so that we have no alternatives).

These actively imposed structures are threefold. They are, first, the essential forms of sense perception, which are space and time. We cannot sense or even imagine anything nonspatial or nontemporal. But that does not mean, for Kant, that the real world actually is spatial and temporal, only that that is the way we have to perceive it.

Second, our concepts are structured by twelve essential logical categories, including substance and accident, cause and effect, necessity and contingency. But these, too, are not objective realities or "things in themselves." They are like cookie cutters in our consciousness that are the forms we impose on the otherwise formless cookie dough of our experience.

Third, we cannot help classifying everything according to the three essential "ideas of pure reason": the ideas of a world (the unity of all phenomena), a self (the unity of all our consciousness), and God (the absolute unifier of self and world). But this is only our necessary way of classifying. None of these can be known (as distinct from being *believed*) to be objectively real, according to Kant; they are constructs of our own consciousness.

This anti-metaphysical epistemology makes impossible an ethics based on metaphysics. Goodness, like being, is our *construct*.

But it can be *rational* (i.e., logical).

Kant begins his ethics by identifying the only good-in-itself as a good will. All other goods—goods of the body, the intellect, and the emotions—are good only when rightly used by a morally right will. Qualities like intelligence, resolution, and happiness, and gifts of good fortune like long life, health, wealth, and power or influence, are not good in themselves, for they can be used for evil by the evil will of a moral monster like Hitler. Think of the self as a ship. The will is the captain of the ship. The intellect is only the navigator, the passions are only the sailors, and the body is only the planks of the ship.

Next, he defines a good will as one that is motivated by moral duty—i.e., respect for moral law. (This is what makes him similar to the Stoics.) That is his answer to the question: What makes a human act morally right?

What makes a human act right is not that it makes you happy and content by satisfying all your desires, as a hedonist would say.

Nor is it that it is appropriate to your situation or circumstances, as a moral relativist would say.

Nor is it that its consequences are desirable, as a utilitarian (see chapter 23) would say—a good end does not justify an evil means.

Nor is it that it obeys a list of the objectively right things rather than wrong things to do (e.g., the Ten Commandments), or that it obeys the will of God, as most religious thinkers would say.

Nor is it that it comes from a virtuous person or makes you into a virtuous person, as an Aristotelian would say.

Nor is it that it is the means to the ultimate end or "greatest good" or goal or purpose or "final cause" or "meaning of life," as Aquinas would say.

What makes a good will good is simply the subjective, personal motive in the will of the actor, and Kant will say that the only moral motive is the motive of moral duty.

Duty is respect for moral law as such, not simply obedience to your social superiors or the desired consequences of obedience, such as happiness.

Kant begins with this premise: the only thing good in itself is a good will. Add to that premise his second premise, that what makes a will good is its moral motive, and you get Kant's conclusion: morality is simply a matter of motive. Doing the right *thing* is not the essence of morality; you must do it for the right *reason* (motive). As St. Thomas Becket says in T.S. Eliot's play *Murder in the Cathedral* when he is tempted to be a martyr out of pride or love of honor and glory, "The last temptation is the greatest treason / To do the right deed for the wrong reason."

But what is the right motive or reason? There is only one. The only truly moral motive is the motive of duty—i.e., respect and obedience to moral law as such. If the will is the only thing that is good in itself, and if a good will is defined by the right motive, then the right motive is the only thing that defines the good in itself, or the absolute good.

What moral law is it, then, that makes a moral choice or act good? It is the single "categorical imperative."

"Imperatives" are commands, and there are two kinds. Hypothetical, or relative, imperatives are expressed with an "if" condition—e.g., if you want to go across the sea, take a boat or a plane; if you want to get an A on the test, study hard. A categorical imperative, by contrast, is unconditional—you absolutely ought to do this and not that. You do it not for consequences or appropriateness or acceptability or happiness (either your own or others') but simply because it is morally right. Hypothetical imperatives are conditional, pragmatic, instrumental, and not morally absolute. Even the principle of Plato and Aristotle that "if and only if you are moral, you will be happy" is a morally compromised and polluted motive in Kant's eyes, because it makes morality instrumental (a means to the end of happiness) rather than absolute.

Kant assumes the modern, subjective meaning of "happiness" here (contentment, satisfaction of desires) rather than the ancient, objective one. Suffering is the opposite of happiness in the modern meaning of "happiness," but suffering can be an ingredient in happiness in the ancient meaning of "happiness," because in that older meaning "happiness" (*eudaimonia*) means perfection or completion of your human nature, and without suffering there is no wisdom, and without wisdom there is no completeness of your humanity.

Kant formulates his single categorical moral imperative in three ways. The first could be called the basic principle of justice, the second the basic principle of charity, and the third the basic principle of freedom.

The first formulation of "the supreme principle of morality" is essentially the Golden Rule, which is clearly known by not only every religion and every culture but even every human being in the world. Its common formulation is "Do unto others what you want others to do to you." Kant's formulation is "Act only according to that maxim [principle] whereby you can at the same time will that it should become a universal law [for all to obey]."

All evil violates this principle. When we hate, kill, steal, or lie, we do not and cannot will that others do the same to us. We make an exception for ourselves: we will that others act morally and refrain from hating, murdering, stealing, or lying, at the very same time as we do that very thing to them. We are thus contradicting ourselves, willing opposite things at the same time.

But although this principle successfully defines all evils, it does not seem to define all goods; for some goods, like choosing marriage, joining the army, or becoming a celibate priest are goods only for some individuals, not all.

The second formulation is to act in such a way that you "treat humanity, whether in your own person or in the person of another, always at the same time as an end and never simply as a means." We must love our neighbors as ourselves, and the essence of love is not a feeling (for feelings cannot be commanded) but a will, goodwill, "to will the good of the other," as Aquinas formulates it. So the moral imperative is to use things (as means) and love people (as ends), not vice versa.

This second formulation can be deduced from the first because we all want to be loved in this essential way, valued for our own sake, not treated merely as instruments; that is why we must do the same to others.

The third formulation is much more controversial. Kant calls it the formula of "autonomy." It is "always to act so that the will could regard itself at the same time as making universal [moral] law." For Kant, true morality cannot originate in another's will, not even a divine Other—that would be "heteronomy," literally "norms from another." Morality must be "autonomous"—i.e., from our own will.

Kant was not an atheist, but (to translate his philosophical point into religious language) he might say that at the Last Judgment we will see ourselves, not God, on the throne. In light of perfect reason, the distinction between our will and God's disappears. For the last and perfect judgment must be by perfect moral reason, and when we judge by reason we judge ourselves by our own participation in eternal, perfect reason. (Perhaps this could be seen as the deeper meaning of "conscience.")

From this third formulation of the categorical imperative, Kant deduces the necessity of free will. If (premise one) there is a categorical imperative, or an absolute "ought"; and if (premise two) "ought implies can" (we do not command machines, or even irrational animals, or judge them morally, or hold them morally responsible); then (conclusion) free will is also absolutely necessary for morality.

Kant also attempts to deduce the moral necessity of a morally perfect God (otherwise the demand for moral perfection is never met and is a mere abstract ideal, not a reality).

He also attempts to deduce the moral necessity for a perfect justice after death (since perfect justice does not exist in this life), and therefore the reality of immortality, or life after death.

Thus, God, free will, and immortality are proven morally rather than metaphysically, practically rather than theoretically. Kant is skeptical of our ability to prove that they are objectively, factually true, but he believes that we can prove that they are morally necessary.

Kant and Aristotle are the two most influential ethical philosophers in history. Perhaps the most concrete difference between the two moral philosophies could be laid out in this example. Imagine a saint (e.g., St. Francis of Assisi) and a notorious sinner (e.g., Al Capone) both choosing to do the right thing (e.g., finding but not keeping someone else's lost wallet containing a fortune). Is there more moral goodness in the right act of the great saint, who makes the right choice easily and habitually and with joy, or in the right act of the great sinner, who makes it with difficulty and painfully, because for him it is purely an act of will since he is tempted by his bad habits? There seems to be a point to both answers.

Some of the most common and most commonsensical objections to Kant are:

1. that he makes no room for moral *habits*—i.e., personal virtues;
2. that he makes no room for emotions or instincts, especially compassion, generosity, gratitude, etc., which almost everyone judges are important aspects of morality;
3. that his moral absolute, duty, should be really only a kind of last resort when higher motives fail. We all judge a mother who does good to her children out of love as a morally better, more complete person than one who does that only out of duty;
4. that if all morality is a matter of duty, what becomes of heroic actions "beyond the call of duty"? Are they not moral? Or is everyone except a hero immoral?
5. that his moral absolutism and rigorism—and this is perhaps the most common objection to Kant—are too demanding for us; that we need non-moral inducements rather than purely moral ones to effectively motivate us. Kant would reply that this is unduly cynical, that everyone responds with admiration

to a pure motive, and that we should not teach morality by non-moral bribes to anyone, not even small children. We all have a moral conscience, and it should be respected, not patronized.

SELECTED BIBLIOGRAPHY

Peter Kreeft, *Socrates Meets Kant*
Immanuel Kant, *Grounding for the Metaphysics of Morals*

23

John Stuart Mill
(AD 1806–1873):
Utilitarianism

Mill's utilitarianism is probably the most influential ethical philosophy in contemporary America.

The most attractive feature of his ethical system is its simplicity. To summarize his whole "bottom line" in three points:

1. Mill identifies a morally good act as one that will produce the best consequences. He is a consequentialist.
2. He identifies the best consequences with "the greatest happiness for the greatest number [of people]." That is his supreme principle of morality, in fact the only one.
3. And he identifies happiness with pleasure. He is a hedonist.

Thus, the three main objections to Mill are the following:

1. This "the end justifies the means" principle is relativistic and seems to justify many things that common sense sees as intrinsically evil—e.g., cannibalism. In a room containing ninety-nine cannibals and one non-cannibal, the greatest happiness for the greatest number would be for the ninety-nine to kill and eat the one.

2. There seems to be no justification for the leap from egotism to altruism. Why should I act for others' happiness and not just for my own? If the only reason is that it makes me happier to do so, my motive then remains as egotistic as before.

3. His hedonism (identifying "good" with pleasure) is not merely a shallow ethics but no ethics at all. Pleasure cannot be the supreme good because it is often a temptation, but virtue is not, and choosing virtue over pleasure is almost the essence of morality. And his psychology of happiness seems as shallow as his ethics, for true happiness requires moral virtue. Success in finding pleasure is not the same as true happiness. Evil, selfish tyrants are not really happy even if they are successful and pleased.

His defenses of his three points are the following:

1. To the charge of relativism, Mill would cheerfully admit that he is a moral relativist, not a moral absolutist like Kant; but he would argue that his distinction between higher and lower pleasures answers the objection from the example of cannibalism, because altruism, love, and cooperation give a higher, more human kind of pleasure to all concerned than mere animal eating.

2. Mill clearly teaches altruism rather than egotism. His justification for this is simply that others' happiness is just as real as one's own. But this presupposes another moral principle—namely, justice. And this brings in another principle than hedonism, for pleasure is always subjective, personal, and individual, while justice is objective, impersonal, and universal. The obvious reason we should not scorn others' happiness and seek only our own is that it is not right, not fair, not just, not true that we and our happiness are more important than others'.

3. And Mill argues that his hedonism is not low, shallow, and animalistic because, unlike his predecessor who invented utilitarianism, Jeremy Bentham, Mill distinguishes qualitatively "higher" pleasures from "lower" ones.

But this means that there must be some higher standard than pleasure with which to judge different pleasures as "higher" or "lower," and therefore it is this rather than pleasure that is the highest good and the highest standard; and this abandons hedonism, which says that pleasure itself is the highest good. Bentham was a more consistent hedonist than Mill.

So Mill's ethical common sense seems to outrun his philosophical principles. This gives Mill himself high marks but his principles low ones.

SELECTED BIBLIOGRAPHY

John Stuart Mill, *Utilitarianism*

Three Existentialists

24

Søren Kierkegaard (AD 1813–1855): The Three Stages on Life's Way

Kierkegaard's "big idea" in ethics is not about the content of ethics—that is for him simply a combination of generic common sense and Kantianism—but about the place of ethics in human life. There are, according to Kierkegaard, three "stages on life's way," which are stages of human, spiritual growth. He calls them "the aesthetic," "the ethical," and "the religious" stages.

The aesthetic stage, which is the stage we are all born into, does not refer to art or the arts but to feeling and experience. It is essentially hedonism, or what Freud calls "the pleasure principle." Usually refined by intelligence and calculation, it seeks pleasure—or, more accurately, power or control, the conquest of boredom by the manipulation of things and people in the world. One who lives in this stage may please other people and conform to social mores and expectations, but he is not truly ethical because his absolute categories, which he uses to judge everything in life, are not ethical good and evil but psychological pleasure and pain, or more exactly, interest and boredom. Little children, Kierkegaard notes, are always well-behaved as long as they are not bored. Aesthetes are neither moral nor immoral but amoral.

Either/Or, Kierkegaard's first book and the one that made him famous, is a series of fictional letters between a brilliant aesthete, Don Juan the Seducer, and an ordinary, responsible, middle-aged judge, William, who urges him on toward the ethical stage through honest self-reflection. For the aesthete really has no self yet; he is simply his relationships to his experiences and to others. He is a series of masks hiding an inner emptiness.

So the "either/or" of the title is not the choice between moral good and moral evil but the choice between ethical choice and no ethical choice; not between morality and immorality but between morality (*and* immorality) and amorality. The question that divides the three kinds of people in the three "stages" is: What essential categories, what opposite options, define your life?

The ethical stage is mature and responsible, unlike the aesthetic stage; but the problem with absolutizing the ethical is that it is boring, abstract, impersonal, and universal, while the aesthetic is attractive because it is interesting, concrete, personal, and individual. Yet the aesthete has no sense of responsibility and really no "I," no self, and no freedom. The aesthete seems to be creative but unfaithful; the ethical person seems to be faithful but not creative. (Kierkegaard's Judge William tries to convince "the seducer" that fidelity is *more* creative, but it is a "hard sell.")

The religious stage solves this dilemma by combining the positive features in each of the other two stages. It is both free and responsible, both individual and altruistic, both creative and faithful. It is essentially a personal relationship of faith (and hope, and love) with God, which motivates one's choices vis-à-vis one's fellow men.

But if this is the God of Christianity, this relationship entails faith in what Kierkegaard calls "the absolute paradox" of the Incarnation, the eternal God entering time; thus, it can be embraced not by reason but only by a "leap of faith."

It is easy for a mere aesthete to appear to be ethical and altruistic if only he amuses and pleases others. It is also easy for a merely ethical person to appear to be religious if only he is a church member and not an atheist and if he behaves ethically. But the essential religious categories are not ethical good and evil but *sin* and *faith*, which are the positive and negative relationships with God, who is a person, not a principle. "Sin" is not just immorality, and "faith" is not just intellectual belief. As faith is like a marriage to God, sin is like divorce or abandonment.

As Kierkegaard explored the contrast between the aesthetic and the ethical in *Either/Or*, he contrasted the ethical and the religious in *Fear and Trembling*, a psychological exploration of the experience of Abraham when God commanded him (at least apparently) to offer up his beloved son Isaac in literal ritual human sacrifice. Kierkegaard calls this a "teleological [for a higher purpose] suspension [for a time] of the ethical"—i.e., the ethical law "thou shalt not kill." It is a change of the categories that determine Abraham's life, from the categories of universal, impersonal ethical good versus evil to the categories of personal faith and obedience versus disobedience.

His point is not that God suspends the ethical for everyone (for usually the religious and the ethical go together), but that everyone's ultimate motive must be either personal faith in God or the choice to adhere to absolute ethical principles. Do you obey God because you obey moral principles, or do you obey moral principles because you obey God? The Christian religion includes a strong ethical dimension (and also a strong aesthetic dimension), but its essence is personal faith, an "I/thou relationship" to a divine person, not an "I/it" relationship to an abstract moral principle, as in Kant.

There is much more to Kierkegaard than this. He is a charming, clever, tricky, and puzzling writer, and he often uses "indirect communication"—i.e., writing from a point of view that is not his own. He is more like a playwright than a typical philosopher.

He is often called the father of existentialism because he always focuses on the concrete life of the existing individual.

SELECTED BIBLIOGRAPHY

Peter Kreeft, *Socrates Meets Kierkegaard*
Robert Bretall, ed., *A Kierkegaard Anthology*

25

Friedrich Nietzsche
(AD 1844–1900):
The Antichrist

Kierkegaard and Nietzsche are often called the two founders of modern existentialism. They both focus on the inner life of the existing individual and his choices; they are both suspicious of abstract reason; and they are both writers of great passion and style. Yet no two philosophers are more totally opposite in what they teach. Kierkegaard said in his last book (*The Point of View for my Work as an Author*) that every sentence he ever wrote was in some way about "becoming a Christian," which was to him the whole meaning of life. Nietzsche called himself "the antichrist" and called Christianity "the greatest of all imaginable corruptions. . . . The most fatal and seductive lie that has ever yet existed. . . . The most repugnant kind of degeneracy that civilization has ever brought into existence. . . . The only unquenchable infamy of mankind." He is certainly the most passionate atheist who ever lived and perhaps the most total and consistent one.

He not only denies but hates everything Christianity affirms as values: God, Christ, love, free will, moral law, compassion, forgiveness, mercy, pity, virtue, sin, faith, reason, humility, justice, democracy, equality, rights, humanism, souls, immortality, heaven, trust, obedience, altruism, reverence, gratitude, sanctity, ordinary people, and even honesty. He questions even "the will to truth," and asks, "Why not rather untruth?" He calls this "the most dangerous question." He exhorts us to go "beyond good and evil" (the title of one of his books) and calls for a "transvaluation of all values."

In *The Genealogy of Morals*, he undermines morality's claim by tracing its origin to the Jews' resentment at their inferiority to their pagan overlords and their invention of moral conscience as a way of equalizing their status in relation to their natural pagan superiors. Sheep naturally want wolves to act more like sheep. Nietzsche says there are two totally different moralities: "slave morality" (for Jews and Christians) and "master morality" (for Nietzscheans). "Slave morality" seeks equality and therefore justice and appeals to reason; "master morality" appeals to superiority and force of will and is authoritarian. But, unlike the Nazis, who selectively used much of his philosophy, especially his "will to power," Nietzsche was not a racist or an anti-Semite, nor did he claim his philosophy was "scientific," as the Nazis did. He would have despised Hitler as a small-minded ruffian. But he would not have been shocked by his immorality.

Like Kierkegaard, Nietzsche focuses on the *status* or *place* of ethics. Ethics is religion's natural partner, and Nietzsche sees these two allied forces as doing more harm to man than anything else in history. Thus, he focuses on Jesus (religion) and Socrates (ethics) as his two primary targets. Like Kierkegaard, he saw Socrates and Jesus as the two most influential men who ever lived, but while they were Kierkegaard's two greatest heroes, they were Nietzsche's two greatest villains. Although Socrates was an agnostic about God, Nietzsche saw his reverence for reason and goodness as the worship of a kind of god without a face.

Nietzsche called Socrates' worship of divine reason "Apollonian," since the Greek god Apollo was the god of the sun, thus light, thus enlightenment, thus reason. And Nietzsche wanted to rehabilitate the worship of Dionysus (passion) instead. Dionysus was the god of the earth, growth, heat, life, grapes, and drunken orgies. In the Greek myth, he was torn apart by the demons of the underworld, and Nietzsche shared the fate of Dionysus when he died after eleven years in an insane asylum, signing his letters "The Crucified."

All of ethics, according to Nietzsche, flattens and squashes us by teaching us to bow, to obey, to conform our will and our lives to something authoritative and superior to ourselves ("the good"); but our destiny, Nietzsche believed, was to overcome this and to become the new God, the "Overman," or "Superman," or "more than man." Nietzsche was thinking in terms of a new species, as new to man as man is to ape.

Nietzsche's magnum opus is *Thus Spake Zarathustra*, a brilliant poetic and prophetic anti-Bible announcing the coming of the next step in (spiritual, not biological) evolution, the next species, the Overman. The Overman has no religion or morality, and he affirms "life" and "the will to power" as self-justifying goods that need no higher justification or judgment and are subject to no higher standards, especially moral standards. They are "beyond good and evil." And so is he. Power for Nietzsche is not a means to any other end beyond itself; it is the end, the whole meaning of life.

When Nietzsche famously announced that "God is dead," he meant, of course, that religious faith is dead. God is not a biological being that can die. Nor, according to Nietzsche, did God ever live outside the fantasies of fools and weaklings who invented him. And now that God is dead, history's purpose can be attained: man can become the super-man, the new God, but only if he wills it. This would be truly "the triumph of the will" (to quote the most effective propaganda film ever made).

Nietzsche is not simply an atheist; he demands to worship something. Like Satanists, he worships power or (more exactly) "the will to power," which he calls "the innermost essence of being." His is a new concept of power: power is not a means to any other end but is its own end. Some (like Lord Acton) say that "all power tends to corrupt, and absolute power corrupts absolutely." Others (like Thomas Aquinas) say that power is "open to good and evil"—i.e., neutral, a usable means to either good or evil ends. Nietzsche says neither: Power is good in itself. Power is God.

We have seen the upshot of this philosophy—first in an insane asylum and then in the ruins of Berlin in 1945. It remains to be seen whether we will see a third version of it on a global scale. If so, we cannot say we had no prophetic warnings.

SELECTED BIBLIOGRAPHY

William Barrett, *Irrational Man*, "Nietzsche"

26

Jean-Paul Sartre
(AD 1905–1980):
The Ethics of Absurdity

I have procrastinated about writing this chapter for weeks, and when I asked myself why, I had to answer that it is because Sartre makes me feel dark, hopeless, and empty. Getting into his world seems like a visit to hell. And this reaction is not atypical. Every one of the few people I know who agree with Sartre's essential philosophy is a dark and troubled soul.

Yet Sartre was one of the most brilliant minds and clearest stylists in history and, at least while he lived, the most famous and popular philosopher in the world, especially among the young.

There are three ways to approach Sartre's ethics. The first is to see it as a deduction from atheism as his premise. He writes, "My existentialism is nothing else but an attempt to draw the full conclusions from a consistently atheistic position." He quotes with approval Dostoevsky's famous saying, "If God does not exist, everything is [morally] permissible"; but while Dostoevsky argued from this premise that since not everything is permissible, therefore God must exist, Sartre argued from the same premise that since God does not exist, therefore everything is permissible.

The second way into Sartre's ethics is to see it as a deduction from his notion of freedom as absolute. Both atheism and absolute freedom seem to be nonnegotiable premises for Sartre. For Sartre, it is either God or freedom, not both. We must choose between an absolute outside us (God) or an absolute inside us (our freedom). Either there is an absolute being (God) who created us and designed us and defined us, and therefore defined and limited our freedom, or we have absolute freedom, but not both.

The third approach that Sartre offers us is an application to ethics of what he himself calls his fundamental insight, the concept of absurdity or meaninglessness. He writes, "Indeed, everything I have ever grasped . . . comes back to this fundamental absurdity." It is not cognitive meaninglessness or a failure of logic but a moral and metaphysical meaninglessness.

Life is a play without a playwright, full of sound and fury but signifying nothing. Meanings and values are subjective, not objective; invented, not discovered; arbitrary, not natural; man-made, not God-made. *And therefore nothing can justify them.*

This may sound like little more than a clever, grown-up version of an adolescent rebellion against all moral authority. But Sartre argues that his philosophy is not an excuse for irresponsibility but the opposite: It does not get us off the hook but on the hook. It makes our responsibility total. Since there is no God, each of us is the God of our world and responsible for the whole of it, especially its values, which are our own invention. Our lives and ourselves cannot be judged by any values or principles from the top down, so to speak. It is just the opposite: all our values and principles are judged by ourselves and our lives, since we created them. Our choices *create* values and therefore judge values rather than values judging our choices.

It logically follows from this that moral argument is impossible. We cannot appeal to universal moral truths, or laws, or principles, for there are none. All we can do is be "authentic," or true to ourselves, or consistent, or non-hypocritical. And even this is only our free choice, so that if I freely choose to be a hypocrite and a liar, Sartre will not argue with me that I am in fact wrong.

There are no wrong choices, since our acts of free choice *create* all rightness and wrongness.

The three central premises of atheism, freedom, and absurdity can be seen to come closely together in the following passage: "My freedom [not God, not human nature, and not moral law] is the unique foundation of values. And since I am the being by virtue of whom values exist, nothing—absolutely nothing—can justify me in adopting this or that value or scale of values. As the unique basis of the existence of values, I am totally unjustifiable. And my freedom is in anguish at finding that it is the baseless basis of values."

This "anguish" also follows directly from Sartre's atheism. It is not a comfortable atheism.

> God does not exist and we have to face all the consequences of this. The existentialist is strongly opposed to a certain type of secular moralism which would like to abolish God with the least possible expense. . . . Something like this: God is a useless and costly hypothesis; we are discarding it; but, meanwhile, in order for there to be an ethics, a society, a civilization, it is essential that certain values should be taken seriously and that they be considered as having an *a priori* existence. . . . The existentialist, on the contrary, finds it very distressing that God does not exist, because all possibility of finding values in a heaven of ideas disappears along with Him; there can no longer be an *a priori* Good since there is no infinite and perfect consciousness to think it.

There are three kinds of atheists. Most modern American atheists are happy or comfortable atheists, whom Sartre criticizes in the above paragraph. Sartre is an unhappy and uncomfortable atheist because he finds no moral meaning. Albert Camus is a third kind of atheist: a moral atheist who is uncomfortable because he finds no God to ground his morality. The protagonist of Camus' novel *The Plague*, the French Doctor Rieux, chooses to stay in Africa to help victims of a terrible plague even though he knows he will probably eventually contract it himself, because even though he is an atheist, he is convinced that the meaning of life is to be a saint. But he also believes that one cannot be a saint without God. He never resolves that dilemma, nor did Camus. He wants to deny Dostoevsky's premise that "if God does not exist, everything is permissible" (which is the equivalent of "you can't be a saint without God"), yet he cannot; and he cannot embrace either God or moral meaninglessness (the denial of which is the equivalent of "the meaning of life is to be a saint").

For those people who are more interested in the practical, lived consequences of a moral system than in the philosophical justification for it, the most disturbing thing about Sartre is not so much his lack of a foundation, whether in God or in anything else, but his description of the kind of life and the kind of human relationships that follow from his philosophy. It is a life in which unselfish love is simply impossible.

Since according to Sartre each of us has the kind of freedom that religion assigns only to God—namely, an absolute freedom— each of us is like the sun at the center of the solar system, and others can only be our planets. There is to me only one "I" (what Sartre calls "being-for-itself"), so there can be no such reality as a "we." That little word that lovers find most meaningful, Sartre finds most meaningless. Others are limits on my freedom. I am my only subject, or "being-for-itself," so they can only be my objects, or "being-in-itself" to me, and I to them. Their gaze upon me turns me into their objects, as my gaze upon them does the same to them. Thus the famous line at the end of his most famous play, *No Exit*: "Hell is other people."

Sartre analyzes gift-giving in an astonishingly cynical way: to give is to control and enslave the recipient of the gift by putting him in your debt. (Remember that next Christmas!) Sartre says that to the truly free person, "nothing comes to him, either from within or from without, that he can receive or accept" without compromising his freedom. There is no such thing as grace, whether from God or from man; no gift, generosity, or goodwill. Thus, the one thing that nearly everyone else but Sartre, whatever else they believe, intuitively senses is life's deepest meaning and value, namely, genuine love for the other—the precious word we whisper to our loved ones as they are dying and the word we long to hear from them when we die—is a lie.

Is that not the perfect definition of the philosophy of hell?

SELECTED BIBLIOGRAPHY

Jean-Paul Sartre, *Existentialism Is a Humanism*
Peter Kreeft, *Socrates Meets Sartre*
Gabriel Marcel, *The Philosophy of Existentialism*, "Existence and Human Freedom"

Two Personalists

27

Gabriel Marcel
(AD 1889–1973):
The Anti-Sartre

Nihilistic philosophers like Sartre are valuable because they are challenges that provoke deeper responses to them, as the Sophists provoked Socrates. Two responses to Sartre are Marcel and Hildebrand.

Marcel is a religious and ethical alternative to Sartre. But instead of deducing his ethics from the premise of God's existence, as Sartre deduces his ethics from the premise of God's nonexistence, Marcel uses the method of phenomenology, which is essentially listening as carefully and open-mindedly as possible to the data of ordinary human experience without prejudices, premises, or presuppositions. (Sartre claims to be a phenomenologist but he is really a rationalist and deductivist.)

Marcel's primary critique of Sartre is that he is not only a reductionist but a nihilist, that he denies "being." Marcel defines "being" as "what withstands—or what would withstand—an exhaustive analysis bearing on the data of experience and aiming to reduce them step by step to elements increasingly devoid of intrinsic or significant value." The signature word for this reductionism is the word "only" or "merely." For Sartre, nearly everything breaks down when analyzed and is less than it appears to be; for Marcel, it is more. As Hamlet says to Horatio: "There are more things in heaven and earth than are dreamt of in your philosophy."

Marcel's most famous and oft-quoted point is the distinction between "problems" and "mysteries." Problems, however complex and difficult they may be, are questions that are solvable in principle because we can abstract ourselves from them and deal with them as impersonal objects. Marcel defines a mystery, by contrast, as "a problem which encroaches upon its own data." That is, mysteries are questions in which we are so involved that abstraction and objectivity are impossible. We cannot recuse ourselves from them. Love, evil, death, suffering, fidelity, hope, and the union of body and soul are examples of mysteries. Philosophers have never adequately solved or resolved them and never will, because they are to philosophy what Heisenberg's uncertainty principle is to physics: the subjective act of observing them makes a difference to what is observed as object. When the actor sees someone in the audience watching him act, that gaze influences and changes the actor himself.

This is why ethics can never be an exact science. We are essentially ethical beings, and our act of thinking about ethics is itself an ethical act. We cannot stand apart from our ethical ideas and evaluate them by non-ethical standards, because the ethical values that make up our very being are the light by which we try to see those ethical values.

Marcel says that the ultimate object of our ethical behavior is always a person rather than a principle, a rule, a law, or a duty. Thus, the ethical good is a "creative fidelity" rather than a submission of our person to something impersonal. "Fidelity is, in reality, the exact opposite of inert conformism. It is the active recognition of . . . a presence. . . . It implies an active and continuous struggle against the forces of interior dissipation, as also against the sclerosis of habit." It is neither an uncreative fidelity to a principle, as in Kant, nor a kind of creative infidelity, free of all principles, as in Sartre.

SELECTED BIBLIOGRAPHY

Gabriel Marcel, *The Philosophy of Existentialism*, "On the Ontological Mystery"
Gabriel Marcel, *Creative Fidelity*
Kenneth Gallagher, *The Philosophy of Gabriel Marcel*

28

Dietrich von Hildebrand
(AD 1889–1977):
Three Kinds of Good
and the Role of the Heart

The most basic term in ethics is "good." Moore and Wittgenstein will both say, for different reasons, that this term is so basic that it is not definable in terms of anything more basic. But even if this is so, the question remains: What kinds of good are there? How is the good divided?

Plato divided it into two: real goods and apparent goods; and he argued that since it is wisdom (moral knowledge) that discriminates between the two, and since we always choose what seems to us to be the real good but which may be only the apparent good, moral virtue is identical with moral knowledge or wisdom. For Hildebrand, that is too simple and rationalistic. If Plato had consulted experience, as phenomenologists like Hildebrand do, he would have found a less simple answer. Hildebrand's answer is that there are three fundamentally different kinds of goods or meanings to the word "good" (and, therefore, its opposite, "bad" or "evil"): the subjectively satisfying, the objective good for the person, and the response to value.

The subjectively satisfying is whatever pleases me or causes me pleasure: physical, emotional, or mental. These may include not only things like tasty food and comfortable sleep but also things that are morally or physically bad, such as the satisfaction that comes from seeing the sufferings of an enemy, or the "high" that comes from drugs, alcohol, or smoking. The subjectively satisfying may include moderate fear (watching a horror movie) or even pain (perhaps to relieve the boredom, or to satisfy masochistic urges). Of this kind of good it is true to say that "there is nothing good or bad but thinking [or feeling] makes it so." It's a "whatever"—whatever turns you on. It is wholly relative and subjective.

A second kind of good is objective: "the objective good for the person" is whatever is really good for you, whatever improves you in any of your dimensions—physically, mentally, emotionally, socially, financially, or in any other way, including morally.

The third and most important kind of good is what Hildebrand calls simply "value." It is what Marcel calls "being"—i.e., *intrinsic* value, not just value to me or for me. Generosity, forgiveness, and justice are examples of *acts* that have intrinsic *moral* value; persons, beautiful works of art, and living things are examples of *things* that have intrinsic *ontological* value.

All values make demands on us; they demand a response appropriate to what they are. We should value animals above rocks, people above animals, love above hate, etc., simply because of what they are. Unlike the first two categories of goods, values are intrinsic, not relative to personal subjects or their desires. We ought to live rightly, to live according to reality—i.e., to give to everything of value the response it deserves. This means to worship God, not human beings or things; to love and respect persons, not things; and to use things, not persons. To live rightly is to give to everything the value response it deserves. It is a kind of three-R principle: Right Response to Reality.

The three categories of good can overlap. A value like love, forgiveness, or generosity, for example, may be subjectively satisfying to us *and* an objective moral good that improves us *and also* a value to which we owe a positive response.

The three-fold distinction helps us to explain why we choose evil. It is not merely ignorance, as Plato thought, nor is it simply preferring a lesser good to a greater good, but it is attending to a lesser *kind* of good: the subjectively satisfying instead of the objective good for the person (e.g., overeating) or instead of an intrinsic value (e.g., winning a game by cheating).

Another distinctive contribution to ethics by Hildebrand is the inclusion of the heart, the seat of love and affection, as well as the rational will in ethics. Traditionally, human acts were divided into the voluntary and the involuntary—i.e., those that were from the rational (intelligent) will and those that were from the feelings or affections—and only the first category was classified as distinctively human, as distinct from the nonrational and unfree animal emotions; thus, they were the only acts for which we were ethically responsible. But Hildebrand notes that some of our spontaneous feelings are also distinctively human, such as gratitude, compassion, and admiration; and ethical common sense rightly regards people who are defective in these feelings as not completely ethical even if their reason is correct and their will is good. Even though the feeling-act is not itself freely chosen, it comes from a person's character, which is rightly judged as morally better or worse. There is something morally missing in the personality of a spontaneously selfish, stingy, or arrogant person, even when that person chooses an act of unselfishness, generosity, or humility out of rational duty alone. Kant's ethic of rational duty would be a good example of such an incomplete ethics. To be a morally good person, one's heart as well as one's reason and will must be trained to good moral habits. If love is a supreme moral value, it needs to be perfected in all its dimensions, the emotional as well as the rational.

Hildebrand's phenomenology explains why this is so. Distinctively human emotions are not just subjective facts in the individual who feels them, like pain and pleasure; they are insights into objective values, glimpses of moral light. They are not just feelings but feelings *about* something, and they can be right or wrong in different degrees, just as acts of intellect or will can be. They are "intentional." They are value responses. One's spontaneous admiration of another person's courage, or one's appreciation of a beautiful work of art, for example, is a value response (ethical or aesthetic) just as much as one's own free choice to do a needed courageous deed or one's own resolution of will to create great art. And we can train these feeling-habits in the same way we can train our will's habits: by practice, by repeated free choices. That is why we are responsible for them.

SELECTED BIBLIOGRAPHY

Dietrich von Hildebrand, *Ethics*
Dietrich von Hildebrand, *The Heart*

Three Analytic Philosophers

29

A.J. Ayer
(AD 1910–1989):
The Meaninglessness
of Moral Propositions

Ayer became famous for one radical little book, *Language, Truth, and Logic*, which, if followed, simply demolishes not only ethics but pretty much all of philosophy, as traditionally conceived, as being cognitively meaningless. Ayer essentially took Hume's conclusions about ethics and translated them into the area of language and logic. His "bottom line" is that ethical judgments are neither true nor false but intellectually meaningless. They are mere expressions of positive or negative feeling, which we mistake for truth claims whenever we argue about moral right and wrong.

Ayer comes to this conclusion from the Humean premise that there are two and only two kinds of truth claims or propositions or declarative sentences: those that can be known to be true or false by the law of noncontradiction alone and those that cannot. The former are tautologies; the latter are verified (shown to be true, either with certainty or probability) or falsified (shown to be false) only by experience, by sense observation. Hume called the former "relations of ideas" and the latter "matters of fact." Examples of the first are "2+2=4," "Red birds are birds," "Nothing is what it isn't," and "If every number is either odd or even, and this number is not odd, then it must be even." Examples of the second are "Boston is in Massachusetts," "Unicorns do not exist," "Book paper burns at 451 degrees Fahrenheit," and "Kennedy was assassinated."

Since these are the only two kinds of propositions that are cognitively meaningful, and since ethical propositions do not fit into either of these two categories, ethical propositions are cognitively meaningless. They are mere expressions of emotion. "Murder is wrong" really means only "I hate murder," and "Generosity is good" really means only "I feel good when I see generosity." Thus, Ayer's theory is sometimes called the "boo-hoorah theory," because it reduces ethical judgments to rooting against or for a favorite sports team.

This is a logical ground for the popular philosophy called "moral relativism," or "moral subjectivism." It is totally "nonjudgmental" and "tolerant." It refuses to "impose" one's own morality (meaning, for Ayer, merely moral *feelings*) on anyone else.

The practical problem with this is obvious: life requires us to make moral judgments—in court, in war, in personal relationships. Value judgments, or ideas of justice and injustice, right and wrong, simply cannot be erased from human life and thought. And even if they could, it would be only by another value judgment: that it is *wrong* to speak of anything as wrong; that judgmentalism must be judged and intolerance not tolerated.

The logical principle Ayer borrows from Hume and uses as the premise from which he deduces his conclusion that ethical propositions are cognitively meaningless is what he calls the "Verification Principle." Nearly all philosophers, including Ayer himself, have rejected it for the very simple reason that it is self-contradictory. If all propositions that do not fit into either one of the two categories (tautologies and empirically verifiable propositions) are meaningless, then the Verification Principle itself is meaningless because it is neither a tautology (self-evident) nor empirically verifiable. It is not self-evident because its contradictory is not self-contradictory, and it is not empirically verifiable because propositions are not empirical entities.

The most usual reason for moral relativism today is not this logical argument of Ayer's but simply the desire not to judge or be judged, to be free from moral categories and "judgmentalism." But of course, a desire is not an argument. We desire riches, long life, pleasure, and a perfect world; that does not mean they will appear. It is obvious that some desires are good (e.g., the desire to set slaves free) and others are not (e.g., the desire to enslave), so desires must be *judged by* some standard of good versus evil, rather than desires *judging* good and evil. Without this "judgmentalism" there is simply no ethics.

SELECTED BIBLIOGRAPHY

A.J. Ayer, *Language, Truth, and Logic*

30

G.E. Moore
(AD 1873–1958):
The Indefinability of "Good"

Moore, who was another of the "analytic philosophers" at Cambridge, along with Ayer, Wittgenstein, and Bertrand Russell, was also, like them, concerned about the analysis of linguistic meaning, but his conclusion about ethics was much more modest than Ayer's: not that goodness, the fundamental ethical category, was *meaningless* or mere subjective emotion, but that it was *indefinable*. It had no definable "nature."

He labeled the idea that it did have a definable nature and could be defined in some other, more basic terms as the fallacy of "naturalism"—whether the "nature of goodness" was defined as knowledge, as in Plato; or the teleological final cause, as in Aristotle; or pleasure, as in hedonism; or utility, as in utilitarianism; or the motive of duty, as in Kantianism. Just as the number one is the basic unit of arithmetic, so goodness is to ethics. All other numbers are defined in terms of "one." But "one" cannot be defined in terms of any other numbers. The process of defining one term in terms of another cannot go on indefinitely; there must be some most basic term, some absolute to which all others are relative.

Thus, Moore calls goodness a "non-natural property." This does not mean it is "supernatural" any more than it means it is sub-natural; for "nature" here does not mean "the universe," but simply "that which can be defined, that which is an answer to the question 'What is it?'"

Moore's point is somewhat similar to Plato's, who also maintained that the ultimate, the "big idea," the "idea of the Good," the essence of Goodness itself, was indefinable, unlike all particular goods like justice or piety or courage. In the *Republic*, he says it can be known only by analogies. It is like the sun: the source of all light is not itself lit up. He also said that it could not be defined because it is infinite—an unusually mystical admission for a rationalistic Greek philosopher.

Moore consistently defended common sense against popular philosophical alternatives to it such as idealism, pragmatism, and skepticism. He would typically write a fifty-page essay of agonizing clarity and excruciatingly careful analysis simply to prove that we do in fact have certain knowledge of some things, such as that we have five fingers on each hand.

SELECTED BIBLIOGRAPHY

G.E. Moore, *Philosophical Studies*

31

Ludwig Wittgenstein
(AD 1889–1951):
Ethics as "Mystical"

Wittgenstein was the most brilliant and admired of the "analytic philosophers." The only book he ever published during his lifetime, the *Tractatus Logico-Philosophicus*, defended a position very similar to Ayer's: that only tautologies and the propositions of science had logical meaning. Yet he said that the whole point of this book was not logic but ethics—even though the word is never mentioned in the book!

What is going on here is a kind of Zen Buddhist *koan* puzzle, a use of words to show what cannot be put into words. The most important sentence in the *Tractatus*, according to Wittgenstein, is the last one: "Whereof one cannot speak, thereof one must be silent." And the main example (though not the only one) of that "whereof one cannot speak," according to Wittgenstein, is ethics. So the book is about ethics by not being about ethics.

In drawing the limits of logical language as narrowly and severely as he did, Wittgenstein aimed to point the reader beyond the book and beyond words to that which, for Wittgenstein, is incomparably more important, which he called "the mystical" (to distinguish it from "the logical"). So it is a point similar to Moore's (that ethics is linguistically indefinable) based on a premise similar to Ayer's (that the limits of the definable are those of the new logic). In fact, in the *Tractatus* he admits that his whole book, like Ayer's, is self-contradictory, since its theory about the limits of language does not itself conform to those limits. He writes, "My propositions are like a ladder." Once the reader climbs up onto the roof, he must throw away the ladder. There is no room for the ladder on the roof. The book eliminates itself, but unlike Ayer's *Language, Truth, and Logic*, it does it deliberately.

Other examples of what Wittgenstein meant by "the mystical" were music (which is not mere sounds that evoke feeling but contains profound meaning that is untranslatable into words), aesthetic propositions (beauty is also indefinable), the self or knowing subject (which cannot at the same time be the known object), and existence itself ("Not *how* the world is, is the mystical, but *that* it is").

So pretty much everything worth saying is unsayable, and pretty much everything sayable is hardly worth saying, except to set off and point out, by contrast, that which transcends language. Wittgenstein himself was fascinated by mystical writers like St. Augustine, Kierkegaard, Angelus Silesius, and Dostoevsky. This puzzled and scandalized his fellow analytic philosophers. It was almost as if he had played a great shaggy dog story joke on them.

How does such a philosophy impact one's life? For Wittgenstein, the point is again the contrast. What he regarded as the most philosophical (wisdom-loving) things he did were (1) to be a gardener in a monastery, (2) to teach Austrian schoolboys, (3) to volunteer for active duty in World War I, and (4) to live as a hermit in a cabin in Norway for a while—all of this more than his academic interaction with the famous philosophers at Cambridge. In his later work, *Philosophical Investigations*, posthumously published, he repudiated almost every major claim of his earlier work in the *Tractatus*, expanding rather than contracting the scope of meaningful language into pragmatic, humanly, and socially relative "language games" and "family resemblances" (essentially analogies), all of which are the polar opposite of his colleagues' attempts to constrict language into a single ideal, mathematically meaningful format.

SELECTED BIBLIOGRAPHY

Ludwig Wittgenstein, *Tractatus Logico-Philosophicus*
Ludwig Wittgenstein, *Philosophical Investigations*

Is Ethics Dead?

32

Alasdair MacIntyre
(AD 1929–):
After Virtue

MacIntyre has passed through many philosophical phases both in his philosophy in general as well as in ethics, which has always been his primary interest: analytic philosopher and phenomenologist, atheist and Catholic, Marxist and Thomist, optimist and pessimist, Nietzschean and Aristotelian, absolutist and relativist. We present here his single most famous and notorious suggestion, the "point" and beginning of his most influential book, *After Virtue*, in his own words, to provoke the reader's reaction and discussion. It is a point as radical and universal as Nietzsche's "transvaluation of all values." It can also relate to the main point of the previous philosopher, Wittgenstein, for what MacIntyre essentially does is add a historical dimension to Wittgenstein's point. Instead of arguing that ethics is in itself not linguistically and logically sayable or thinkable, MacIntyre argues that it always was but no longer is.

After the excerpt from MacIntyre, we present a contrary and more traditional and optimistic position from Aquinas, who argues that the knowledge of the natural moral law is innate and not abolishable from the human heart.

MacIntyre begins by narrating the plot of the apocalyptic science fiction classic *A Canticle for Leibowitz* by Walter M. Miller Jr. and using it as an analogy for his ethical thought experiment:

> Imagine that the natural sciences were to suffer the effects of a catastrophe. A series of environmental disasters are blamed by the general public on the scientists. Widespread riots occur, laboratories are burnt down, physicists are lynched, books and instruments are destroyed. Finally a Know-Nothing political movement takes power and successfully abolishes science teaching in schools and universities, imprisoning and executing the remaining scientists. Later still there is a reaction against this destructive movement and enlightened people seek to revive science, although they have largely forgotten what it was. But all that they possess are fragments: a knowledge of experiments detached from any knowledge of the theoretical context which gave them significance; parts of theories unrelated either to the other bits and pieces of theory which they possess or to experiment; instruments whose use has been forgotten; half-chapters from books, single pages from articles, not always fully legible because torn and charred. Nonetheless all these fragments are reembodied in a set of practices which go under the revived names of physics, chemistry, and biology. Adults argue with each other about the respective merits of relativity theory, evolutionary theory, and phlogiston theory, although they possess only a very partial knowledge of each. Children learn by heart the surviving portions of the periodic table and recite as incantations some of the theorems of Euclid. Nobody, or almost nobody, realizes that what they are doing is not natural science in any proper sense at all. . . .
>
> In such a culture men would use expressions such as "neutrino," "mass," "specific gravity," "atomic weight," in ways which would resemble in lesser or greater degrees the ways in which such expressions had been used in earlier times before

scientific knowledge had been so largely lost. But many of the beliefs presupposed by the use of these expressions would have been lost, and there would appear to be an element of arbitrariness and even of choice in their application which would appear very surprising to us. What would appear to be rival and competing premises for which no further arguments could be given would abound. Subjectivist theories of science would appear. . . .

This imaginary world is very like one that some science fiction writers have constructed. We may describe it as a world in which the language of natural science, or parts of it at least, continue to be used but is in a grave state of disorder. . . .

The hypothesis which I wish to advance is that in the actual world which we inhabit the language of morality is in the same state of grave disorder as the language of natural science in the imaginary world which I described. What we possess, if this view is true, are the fragments of a conceptual scheme, parts which now lack those contexts from which their significance derived. We possess indeed simulacra of morality, we continue to use many of the key expressions. But we have—very largely, if not entirely—lost our comprehension, both theoretical and practical, of morality. . . .

For the catastrophe will have to have been of such a kind that it was not and has not been—except perhaps by a very few—recognized as a catastrophe.

Aquinas' response (from *Summa theologiae* 1-2.94.2–6):

There is in man an inclination to good, according to the nature of his reason, which nature is proper to him. . . .

The [knowledge of the] natural law is the same in all men. . . .

The natural law is common to all nations. . . .

It is . . . evident that as regards the general principles . . . of practical [moral] reason, truth . . . is the same
for all and is equally known by all. . . . But as to the proper
conclusions of the practical reason, truth is not the same for
all nor is it equally known by all. . . . This principle will be
found to fail the more according as we descend further into
detail. . . . Consequently we must say that the natural law, as
to general principles, is the same for all. . . . But as to certain
matters of detail, which are conclusions, as it were, of those
general principles, it is the same for all in the majority of
cases . . . yet in some few cases it may fail . . . since in some the
reason is perverted by passion or evil habit . . . thus formerly,
theft, although it is expressly contrary to natural law, was not
considered wrong among the Germans [Gypsies]. . . .

Whether the natural law can be abolished from the heart
of man? . . . Augustine says: "The law is written in the hearts of
men, which iniquity itself effaces not." . . . As to those general
principles, the natural law, in the abstract, can nowise be blotted out from men's hearts. But it is blotted out in the case of a
particular action insofar as reason is hindered from applying
the general principle to a particular point of practice, on
account of concupiscence or some other passion. . . . But as to
the other, i.e., the secondary, precepts, the natural law can be
blotted out from the human heart . . . by vicious customs and
corrupt habits as among some men theft, and even unnatural
vices, as the Apostle says (Rom. 1), were not esteemed sinful.

I rarely win when I disagree with Aquinas. He is a formidable
"Summa" wrestler. Yet my experience in teaching freshmen seems
to confirm MacIntyre's point. For the philosopher my students
always flunk the easiest tests on is Aristotle, of all people, and
the reason is essentially their inability to comprehend a single
term: "nature" or "form." They cannot wrap their minds around
the utterly traditional and utterly unmodern notion that moral

as well as physical things have essential natures or "forms" that are unchangeable; that there is an unalterable natural order in morality; and that some acts are therefore wrong because they are *unnatural* (not just *uncommon*), in sexuality as well as in other areas of human life.

I will now add a paragraph that is so "politically incorrect" that it will probably cost me thousands of dollars in royalties for this book, simply because I want to say what I honestly believe to be true.

The clearest example of MacIntyre's point is the historically unprecedented, radical, sudden, and nearly total change in public opinion concerning homosexuality and same-sex marriage. Until recently, that was the stock example of an unchangeable and obvious moral wrong (thus Aquinas' word "even" in his last sentence). But to state what all cultures throughout history believed on this issue today is to commit "hate speech" and to disenfranchise oneself from all possibility of rational argument in the minds of the "educated."

This issue also exemplifies how difficult modern academics find it to sharply distinguish the acceptance or rejection of a passionately believed *idea* from the acceptance or rejection (judgment) of a *person*. Especially on this issue, it is felt to be impossible to "love the sinner and hate the sin." Why?

SELECTED BIBLIOGRAPHY

Alasdair MacIntyre, *After Virtue*

Conclusion

A conclusion is supposed to be an ending, but having finished this book, you are now only at a beginning. This book is for beginners. (So was St. Thomas Aquinas' three-thousand-page masterpiece, the *Summa theologiae*!) So it is now time to begin thinking about ethics, specifically about the "big ideas" that the big minds of the past have deposited in our mental bank accounts. What are we going to do with them?

The first thing to do with them is to understand them. If we do not understand them, our attempts to argue about them and evaluate them will not really be about *them* but about our own misunderstandings of them. One very simple and obvious way to understand them better is to reread them more slowly, carefully, and thoughtfully.

The second thing to do with them is to evaluate them. And this means four things:

1. to identify and understand the reasons for each "big idea" in the mind of the philosopher who proposed it;
2. to evaluate those reasons;
3. to identify and understand the reasons other philosophers have for not agreeing with it; and
4. to evaluate those reasons.

And in understanding and evaluating reasons and arguments, always remember that there are three and only three checkpoints for any argument:

1. First, are there any terms used ambiguously? Does any term change its meaning in the course of the argument?
2. Second, are there any false premises?
3. Third, are there any logical fallacies? Does the conclusion necessarily follow from the premises?

A third thing to do with these "big ideas" is to apply them; that is, to ask the question: If we accept the idea as true, what difference would this make to our ethical thought and action? How might the idea apply to a contemporary controversy or problem, either personal or global?

I wish you all an exciting and profitable journey down the roads of ethical philosophizing!

Appendix I:
220 Questions

Here are some questions for discussion and argument, either in live debates or in original argumentative essays, on the 32 philosophers' "big ideas." You may want to read a more complete account of the philosophers first, beginning with a history of philosophy for beginners, *Socrates' Children: An Introduction to Philosophy from the 100 Greatest Philosophers*, in four volumes, by the author. Especially challenging questions that invite longer essays are starred (*).

THE OLDEST ETHICAL TEACHER

1. If the universal or nearly universal belief in a real moral law (Logos, Tao, or Ṛta) is true, why is this law so often denied by modern thinkers, both philosophers and ordinary people?
2. If it is not true, why did all or nearly all premodern thinkers, both philosophers and ordinary people, believe it?
3. How would you try to prove the reality of this *Logos* to someone who denied it?
4. How would you try to disprove the reality of this *Logos* to someone who believed it?

HINDUISM

1. Can ethics be based on "the wants of man"? Are "wants" the same as desires? How can "wants" be distinguished from "needs"? Can ethics be based on human "needs"? Why or why not?

2. How can you distinguish natural wants or needs from non-natural or artificial ones? How are mistakes possible here?

*3. Are there any other wants or needs that are natural or inherent in universal human nature besides the four distinguished by the Hindu tradition? If so, list and justify them.

4. By what standard can you rank the wants or needs of man in a hierarchy?

BUDDHA

1. How would a Buddhist try to persuade a non-Buddhist that Nirvana is real and desirable?

2. If Nirvana, or Buddha-consciousness, is mystical and not rational, and if it transcends all the distinctions made by ordinary consciousness, how can it motivate the apparently very distinctive ethical and moral behavior that enlightened Buddhists manifest?

3. How can there be unselfish thoughts, motives, or acts such as are recommended and often achieved in Buddhism if there is no real individual self behind them, as Buddhism teaches? Must there not be a self to choose either selfish or unselfish thoughts, motives, or acts? On the other hand, if the ego is real, how can an ego be egoless, and how can a self be unselfish?

4. Why is there nearly universal agreement that the human self's fulfillment, good, happiness, and duty is to be unselfish?

5. Is there an essential difference between (a) selflessness, or unselfishness, as the *absence* of selfishness (egotism), and (b) the active presence of unselfishness as a positive attitude or motive?

6. Is there a difference between compassion (*karuna*) and love (*agape*, or "charity")? If so, what is it?

*7. Test the applicability of the four-step logical form of Buddha's practical analysis (symptoms, diagnosis, prognosis, prescription) by applying it to the ethics of different thinkers (e.g., Socrates, Jesus, Machiavelli, Hobbes, Rousseau, Marx, Freud, Homer Simpson, etc.).

8. If the fourfold pattern in the previous question (7) holds true for both the material and the immaterial, why? Why is there such a close parallel between a physical doctor's analysis of the body and the analysis of a "spiritual doctor" like Buddha or any of the other thinkers mentioned? Why do so many physical analogies work for nonphysical things (e.g., ignorance as "blindness," wickedness as a moral "disease," the virtuous "golden mean" as a balance of spiritual forces like the balance of chemicals in the body)? They obviously do work, but why?

9. What is the connection or relationship between materialism and atheism? How tight is it? Is the connection necessary? Why or why not? And what is the connection or relationship between believing in some immaterial or spiritual reality and some sort of religion? Is the connection necessary or unnecessary?

CONFUCIUS

1. Confucianism has always been a successful social system in China, while Taoism never has been. What does this fact prove or not prove?

2. To most Westerners, Taoism is much more interesting than Confucianism, and the *Tao Te Ching* one of the most interesting and controversial books ever written, while Confucius' *Analects* is probably the most boring and platitudinous religious book ever written. What does this indicate about readers in the West?

3. Although Lao Tzu and Confucius did not understand or agree with each other at all, and though their philosophies are in stark contrast in many ways, China has traditionally achieved some sort of synthesis of the two. What does that say about China? Is such a synthesis Taoistic? Is it Confucian? How?

4. In China, artists are typically more Taoist than Confucian, while politicians are typically more Confucian. Also, Taoists are usually individualists while Confucians are communitarians. Why? Is this difference proper to China only, or the East only, or ancient times only, or is it also true of the modern West?

5. Why has Lao Tzu's political advice ("Govern big countries like you cook little fish") never worked on a large scale? Why has the more "legalistic" Confucianism worked so well?

LAO TZU

1. For Lao Tzu, nothing in nature fails to follow the Tao except foolish human beings. How can the same Tao be both a choice—i.e., a human option (it characterizes the lives of sages but not fools)—and a natural necessity? Why is there no foolishness in nature? Isn't violence foolish? And isn't nature full of violence?

2. How can the very same reality (the Tao) be both transcendent and immanent, invisible and visible, eternal and temporal? Aren't those opposites exclusive of each other?

*3. Compare Lao Tzu's *Tao Te Ching* with Jesus' "Sermon on the Mount" (Matt. 5–7). You will probably find some strong similarities and some strong differences.

*4. Compare what Lao Tzu says about Tao with what the Jewish and Christian Scriptures say about God (you will find both strong similarities and strong differences).

MOSES

1. What did Moses (or God) mean by the commandment to "love" both God and neighbor?
2. The Jewish religion united the moral instinct and the religious instinct much more closely than any other ancient tradition. Why has this survived and become nearly universal in Western civilization? Why does everyone expect a religion to foster morality even if they do not believe the religion?

JESUS

1. Jesus' most famous sermon, the "Sermon on the Mount," summarizes his moral teachings. Yet it seems impossibly idealistic and perfectionist and unlivable. Is that so? If not, why not? If so, why is it so popular?
2. Does Jesus' ethic of *agape* unite the "duty ethics" of Kant and the "happiness ethics" of Aristotle, or does it transcend them both instead of uniting them? Can it do both? Explain.
3. Is this ethic "simple" or "complex"? Can it be both? If so, how, if "simple" and "complex" are mutually exclusive? What is the difference between "simple" and "simplistic"?

MUHAMMAD

1. Muslims, unlike Jews and Christians (and most secularists), believe that religious revelation is political as well as personal, that God revealed to Muhammad principles of an ideal social and political order for all mankind. What is the rational and empirical evidence (as distinct from arguments from religious authority and scriptures) both for and against that claim?
2. Why are most religious people who are not Muslims moral absolutists and political relativists? Why are most Muslims both moral and political absolutists? Why are most secularists both moral and political relativists?

3. Is there any reconciliation possible between the Ash'arites and the Mu'tazilites, or between Euthyphro and Socrates? How did Thomas Aquinas mediate between these two positions?

4. What are the consequences of these three options (Ash'arite voluntarism, Mu'tazilite rationalism, and a mediating position) for a "natural law" morality such as that of Aquinas?

5. How crucial is the metaphysical issue of nominalism versus realism (concerning universals such as justice) to this ethical issue? Is it a philosophical issue or a religious issue that divides most Muslims from most non-Muslims on the relation between faith and reason, religious revelation and philosophical wisdom?

6. Islam originally spread by military conquest rather than merely by personal conversion; and throughout its history, as today, Islam has fostered many wars and continues to do so. However, (a) the vast majority of Muslims stand against terrorism; (b) the notion of *jihad* (holy war) in the Quran applies first of all to the individual's spiritual war against sin in his own life; and (c) other religions, especially Christianity, also have a spotted history of religious warfare. Is this an inevitable feature of Islam or is it changeable without compromising essential Muslim principles? (Perhaps this is a question for Muslims only.)

SOCRATES

1. Would you like to have Socrates as your brother or your roommate? Why or why not? (You should read some of his dialogues before answering this question.)

*2. Of the three paradoxes mentioned, which seems to you the most nearly right? Why? Which seems the most nearly wrong? Why?

3. All three paradoxes ignore the body. Why do you suppose Socrates did that? Is there both something wise and also something foolish there? If so, what?

4. How would you define the role of wisdom in morality?

5. If you had to choose between suffering a great evil (say, torture) and doing it (to someone else, who is innocent), which choice would you make? Why? (The question is not your psychological prediction about how courageous and heroic you would probably be under torture, but whether you in principle agree with Socrates' second paradox or not.)

6. What difference, and how much of a difference, does the existence or nonexistence of life after death make to the third paradox?

7. Are there, as Socrates believed, timeless and unchangeable laws of morality? If so, does that prove that there must be a God? What is the relation between an eternal divine lawgiver and an eternal moral law? If God is the only foundation for such a law, why do many intelligent unbelievers, agnostics, and even atheists believe in such a law?

*8. If you believe that the existence of God and the existence of objective moral law are both true, or probable, or even possible, do you think that an act is morally good because God wills it or that God wills it because it is morally good? Why? How would someone who believes the opposite answer defend it and argue against yours? (Read Plato's *Euthyphro* for a Socratic dialogue on this subject.)

PLATO

1. Some say Plato betrayed Socrates by applying his principles to politics in the *Republic*. Do you agree or not? Why?

2. Plato also tried to give Socrates' ethics a metaphysical foundation in his Theory of Forms, or Theory of Ideas. Do you think this kind of thing is necessary or not? Why?

3. Why do you think Plato's individual ethics and psychology has been more influential than his politics?

4. Why do you think there have been thousands of saintly individuals but no saintly states?

5. Do you think the ethics and moral values of the state ought to be parallel to those of the individual or not? Why?

6. What is the difference between an idea and a Platonic Idea? What is your evaluation of Plato's Theory of Forms (Ideas), especially its inversion of the expected relation between ideas and things: that things are images of Ideas rather than Ideas being images of things?

*7. Do you believe that "justice is always more profitable than injustice" both for states and for souls, as Plato tries to prove in the *Republic*? Why or why not? (Remember to define what you mean by "profitable." Obviously Plato did not mean "producing monetary profit" or even "producing temporary subjective feelings of satisfaction and contentment." What did he mean?)

8. Do you agree with Plato that "it is better to suffer evil than to do it"? Why or why not? Do you agree that virtue is the only thing you need for true happiness (blessedness)? Why or why not? Does Aristotle agree with either or both of these two ideas? Why or why not?

ARISTOTLE

1. Why do you think people today mean by "happiness" something subjective (a feeling of satisfaction, of contentment) while most of the ancients (e.g., Plato and Aristotle) meant something objective (blessedness)?

2. What do you think is the relation between suffering and happiness? Would you be happier if you never suffered?

3. Evaluate Aristotle's idea that each virtue is a "golden mean" between two extremes (opposite vices).

*4. Aristotle, like Plato, bases his ethics on two metaphysical assumptions that most premodern philosophers believed and most modern philosophers don't: that things have a "formal cause," a "nature," an "essence" as opposed to "accidents," and that there are "final causes" (ends, goals, purposes, designs, goods) that are objectively real, not just subjective thoughts and desires. (1) Evaluate these two assumptions. (2) What difference does each make to ethics? (3) Why do you think most ancient philosophers believed them and most modern philosophers do not?

5. Aristotle's ethics is usually called a "virtue ethics" because it sees personal virtue as the determining factor in achieving life's true good: happiness, or blessedness. (Aristotle began with Plato's four "cardinal virtues" and added about a dozen more.) Do you see any advantages or disadvantages in this "virtue ethics" in contrast with the two major modern alternatives of utilitarianism (calculating consequences and seeking "the greatest happiness for the greatest number") and Kantian rule-based or principle-based ethics (e.g., the Golden Rule)?

6. Aristotle does not base his ethics on a deduction from any self-evident absolute principles, or on the existence of Platonic Forms and the Idea of the Good, or on the existence of a morally perfect being or God. Does this make him a relativist? Why or why not?

7. Does Aristotle's doctrine of the "golden mean" make him a moral relativist? Why or why not?

8. What are the advantages and disadvantages of centering ethics on (personal) *virtue(s)*, as Aristotle does, rather than impersonal *laws*, as Kant does?

9. Which of these two options (question 8) do you think is more naturally allied with religious theism? Why?

PROTAGORAS

1. In what sense, if any, do you agree and in what sense do you disagree with Protagoras' dictum that "man is the measure of all things"?

2. Could one be an honest and morally serious Sophist and relativist? Why or why not?

*3. Imagine how Protagoras would answer the six objections at the end of the chapter. Then imagine how you might answer Protagoras' answers. (It is important to understand both sides of important and controversial issues!)

EPICURUS

1. What do you see as the *relationship* between (a) physical pleasure, (b) pleasure as such, (c) being pleased, (d) happiness, (e) blessedness (in Aristotle's sense of *eudaimonia*), (f) moral duty, and (g) moral heroism? (Think carefully about this question before answering it!)
2. Do you see any other problems with hedonism besides egotism?
3. Do you see any way to answer the objection that hedonism cannot explain or justify altruism?
4. Compare, in your own experience, the times you succeeded in creating a kind of Epicurean garden for yourself and the times you could not or would not do so. What was the result each time? Why?
5. Why does the text say it is "fortunate" that Epicurus never married or had children?

EPICTETUS

1. Why do you think Stoicism was the most popular philosophy in the Roman Empire?
2. The most popular critique of Stoicism is that it seems to suppress love and compassion. If that is true, and if nearly everyone in modern Western civilization prizes love and compassion (more than our ancestors, who seem, by comparison, quite primitive, tough, and cruel), why is Stoicism fairly popular today?
3. How is Buddhism similar to Stoicism? How are they different?
4. If you had to choose between adopting either Stoicism or Epicureanism as your philosophy of life, which would you choose and why?

5. Why is it often said that dogs are Epicureans and cats are Stoics?

6. Is that the same question as: What would you rather be, a slob or a snob? Granted that both are unfair caricatures of these two philosophies, which is the more unfair and why?

*7. Would you rather be a Stoic with an Epicurean friend or an Epicurean with a Stoic friend? Why?

8. It's sometimes said that Epicureans deal with pleasure very well but can't deal with pain, and Stoics deal with pain very well but can't deal with pleasure. How accurate is that critique? Does this help you decide your answer to any of the questions 1 through 7 above?

9. The Stoics claimed to be disciples of Socrates, especially of his conviction that "no evil can happen to a good man." Evaluate this claim.

AUGUSTINE

1. If the God Augustine believes in exists, does it necessarily follow that Augustine is right in *The City of God* in dividing the human race into the two "cities"? Why or why not?

*2. Augustine's most famous argument for God is his life, his experience, which is summarized in the single sentence "Thou hast made us for thyself, and [that is why] our hearts are restless until they rest in thee." This is a causal argument, tracing the effect (our restlessness, our discontent with this imperfect world) to its cause (our having been designed with a God-sized and God-shaped hole in our heart). How would an opponent challenge Augustine's argument? Ambiguous term, false premise, or invalid logic? How would Augustine reply?

3. Let us recast the argument in the way made famous by C.S. Lewis. Major premise: All natural, innate, internal, universal desires correspond to realities that are their objects and that can satisfy them. For every hunger there is a food (truth,

sex, friendship, pleasure, beauty, love, etc.). But we all have a natural, innate desire for a perfect being (God) and a perfect world (heaven) and a perfect relationship with that being (eternal bliss). Therefore, God and heaven exist. Evaluate this argument by the three checkpoints above in the conclusion.

4. What difference does the premise of this argument (our discontent and desire for more) make to ethics?

5. What difference does its conclusion (God) make to ethics?

ANSELM

1. Are you a defender or a critic of Anselm's "ontological argument" for God? Why?

2. Does this book's recasting of Anselm's argument into ethical terms work? That is, (1) does it successfully define the greatest good, and (2) does it prove its existence?

3. What difference does it make here and now if you agree with Anselm about our ultimate end? (See the last two paragraphs.)

AQUINAS

1. Summarize and evaluate Aquinas' basic answer to the question of the relationship between religious faith and philosophical reason. (The less vague and the more clear and specific you are in summarizing his answer, the more adequate your evaluation will be.)

2. Aquinas defines a law as an "ordinance" or command, thus implying a will. Yet he says it is an ordinance of "reason." Is that a contradiction? What is the relation in his mind between the reason and the will of the lawmaker (whether divine or human)?

*3. Why, in our society today, is Aquinas' idea of a natural moral law more controversial and more threatening to those who disagree with it than his idea of eternal law or the divine law?

4. How important is the fact that most intellectuals today reject a natural moral law? How important is it that most intellectuals

223

in all previous societies believed in some form of it? Has this book exaggerated this disagreement?

5. Do you think there are any other virtues that are as important as, or more important than, the seven that Aquinas lists? If so, which and why?

6. How has the word "virtue," or at least its connotation, changed since Aquinas' day?

7. What other candidates for life's greatest good would you add to Aquinas' list of eight?

8. Aquinas has two kinds of arguments for God, one from the causal order of the universe and its inability to be explained without a first cause or ordering mind, and the other one from practical human life and its inability to satisfy the deepest desires of our hearts without a supreme good (God). What are the strengths and weaknesses of each argument? Which is more persuasive to you? Why?

MACHIAVELLI

1. Almost no one denies that Machiavelli is not "one of the good guys." And almost no one denies that history shows there are plenty of "bad guys" who have a lot of power and cleverness. Neither of those points is controversial. So what, exactly, is controversial about Machiavelli?

2. The chapter begins by summarizing the Machiavellian revolution this way: "Machiavelli effectively put an end to the application of ethics to politics." What are the most important assumptions behind his new idea that ethics cannot be applied to politics, and what are the most important assumptions behind the previous idea that it can? Is it a difference between two opposing views of ethics, of politics, or of both?

*3. Compare and contrast Machiavelli's division of life into *virtu* and *fortuna* with the Stoics' division of life into "what can be changed" and "what cannot be changed." If the division is the same for both schools of thought, why do Stoics and

Machiavellians draw such opposite conclusions from this common principle?

4. Plato's idealism has always been more popular when applied to individuals than when applied to politics, as he did in the *Republic*. Machiavellianism has always been more popular when applied to politics than when applied to individual lives. Why is that?

5. If part of the answer to the above question is that "politics is the art of compromise," why do most people believe that compromise is (a) more necessary and (b) more ethically justifiable in politics than in individual life? (By the way, do not let that quotation that "politics is the art of compromise" suffice for your answer to question 4; what is the other part of your answer?)

6. How would you reply to Machiavelli's argument that "it is better to be feared than loved" (par. 5)? If you've seen the movie *A Bronx Tale*, which is about that very quotation, how does the movie treat that question?

HOBBES

1. Is the derivation or deduction of Hobbes' ethics from his metaphysics a *necessary* one? Could one embrace Hobbes' metaphysical premise (materialism) without his ethical conclusions? Could one embrace his ethical conclusions without his metaphysical premise? Why or why not?

2. What are the essential arguments for and against Hobbes' materialism in metaphysics?

3. What are the essential arguments for and against the conclusions Hobbes draws from his metaphysical premise of materialism?

4. Why do you think ethically "shocking" philosophers like Machiavelli and Hobbes are so popular? Why do you think their positions are often more widely popular today than they were in their own lifetimes?

5. How do you think Hobbes would answer the "argument from experience" in the last paragraph? If he is an empiricist, who judges all reasoning by experience, why does he seem to impose a one-sided ideology onto the common experience of human nature as neither simply selfish nor simply unselfish?

ROUSSEAU

*1. Rousseau is obviously the opposite of Hobbes in many ways (I listed six); is there any common *principle* (not the "bottom line" *conclusion* of some kind of totalitarianism) that he shares with Hobbes, when both are compared to the older ethical tradition? Compare Aristotle with both.

2. Do you see anything common to Hobbes and Rousseau in their notion of freedom? In their notion of reason? In their notion of the role and power of the passions, feelings, emotions, and desires?

3. Hobbes is a "hard," scientific thinker; Rousseau is a "soft," unscientific or even anti-scientific thinker. Do you see any way in which they are both influenced by the new science? Science cannot, apparently, deal with ethics (moral values do not register on any strictly quantitative and empirical scientific scale), yet its influence can change our attitude toward ethics. How?

4. Would you rather live in a Hobbesian society or in a Rousseauian one? Why?

HUME

1. What is the obvious argument from moral *experience* against Hume's "emotivist theory of values"? Think: When you have to choose between paying the taxes you justly owe and cheating the government by lying on your tax form so that you can enjoy that expensive vacation you always wanted, is morality an *emotion*? Hume claims to be an empiricist (all knowledge is based on experience); is this what you experience when you

make that choice? (Be honest! The question is about your experience, not your principles.)

2. Why do empiricists like Hume more often tend to believe the emotivist theory than rationalists like Descartes or Plato? Why does that seem to be paradoxical? (Cf. the first sentence in question 1.)

*3. Empiricists tend toward materialism in metaphysics because of their epistemology (Why?), while rationalists do not (Why?). How does one's metaphysics determine one's epistemology? How does one's epistemology determine one's metaphysics? How does one's metaphysics determine one's ethics? How does one's epistemology determine one's ethics? Does one's ethics determine one's metaphysics? Does one's ethics determine one's epistemology?

4. What is the attraction in Hume's ethics? Why is it more attractive today than in the past? Why is it attractive for teenagers but not for married people, especially with children? Why is it often associated with "liberalism" rather than "conservatism" in contemporary America?

5. An obvious objection to the emotivist theory of values is its natural *consequence* in life. To see this, refer again to the example in question 1. Is this consequence an attraction of the theory, an objection to it, or both?

6. When you are about to express a moral judgment, why does prefacing it with "I feel that . . ." feel better than "I think that . . ."? Does it also "think" better? If not, and you have to choose from the beginning between "I feel that" and "I think that," aren't both choices arbitrary and unprovable? And if so, doesn't that make it decidable only by strength of feeling rather than by thinking?

7. If values are feelings, how do you account for the fact that we often make a moral choice to follow the weaker feeling rather than the stronger one? (See again the example in question 1 above.)

KANT

1. In the beginning of this chapter, Kant is summarized as combining the essential objective and typically premodern good with the essential subjective and typically modern good. Is this possible without contradiction? Why or why not?

2. Is there another way to achieve this combination besides Kant's way? Does Aquinas to it? Does Hildebrand?

3. What is the advantage and what is the disadvantage of Kant's strategy of not grounding ethics in metaphysics?

4. Could one agree with Kant's ethics without agreeing with his metaphysics and epistemology (his "Copernican Revolution in philosophy")? Why or why not?

5. Is there a significant difference between basing morality on a single absolute "categorical *imperative*" or *law* and basing it on a single absolute *good* or *end* (final cause)?

6. If morality is based on a final cause or end, as in Aristotle and Aquinas, does this mean it can contain only hypothetical imperatives rather than categorical imperatives? Why or why not? Does it depend on whether one uses Aristotle's notion of happiness as objective blessedness or Kant's as subjective satisfaction of inclinations? If so, how? If not, why not?

7. Must morality be based on a single good, end, or law? Can there be many moral absolutes? Why or why not?

8. Evaluate the *logic* of the steps of Kant's analysis beginning with the principle that the only good in itself is a good will and ending with the first formulation of the categorical imperative.

9. Are there three categorical imperatives or only three formulations of the one and the same categorical imperative? Why?

10. Does Kant's conclusion that morality is only a matter of motive—a conclusion most premoderns would disagree with—logically follow from the two premises that (1) only a good will is good in itself and that (2) what makes a good

will good is its motive? If so, and if you disagree with the conclusion, which premise do you disagree with and why?

11. Evaluate Kant's principle that the only truly moral motive is duty (respect for moral law). When we do a great good to another person, often at great expense to ourselves, do we act out of moral duty, out of personal inclination, out of our will for the other's good, or all three? If all three, do all three have moral worth? If so, why does Kant restrict moral worth to the first of these three factors?

12. Does Kant's second formulation of the categorical imperative logically depend on the first? If so, why? If not, what other premise could it follow from?

13. Does Kant's first formulation of the categorical imperative necessarily lead to the second? Why or why not? (Notice that questions 11 and 12 are logically different.)

14. Granted that the first formulation of the categorical imperative defines all moral evils but not all moral goods, how could Kant account for the many moral goods that are not defined by it?

15. Does the second formulation of the categorical imperative also identify all evils but not all goods? Why or why not?

16. Do any of the three formulations of the categorical imperative account for duties to God as well as to neighbor? Why or why not?

17. Evaluate Kant's third formulation of the categorical imperative and Kant's argument that it logically follows from the other two.

18. Can the third formulation be interpreted in a way compatible with traditional theism, or are they mutually exclusive?

19. What other arguments for God, for free will, and for the immortality of the soul are there? Do you think they are stronger or weaker than Kant's moral argument for them? Why?

20. When evaluating the example of Al Capone versus St. Francis, common sense instinctively responds both in a pro-Kantian way (Capone's act has more moral worth because it costs him more effort) and in an anti-Kantian way (Francis' act has more moral worth because it flows from a better person). How would you reconcile these two opposite reactions?

*21. How would Kant respond to each of the criticisms at the end of the chapter?

MILL

1. Is utilitarianism attractively simple? Or is it unattractively simplistic? Is "simple" good or bad in ethics? What's the difference between "simple" and "simplistic"?

2. *Must* there be one supreme principle of morality, as there is for thinkers as diverse as Augustine, Kant, and Mill? Why or why not?

3. Can there be a non-hedonist utilitarianism? Why or why not?

4. *Why* is altruism a problem for utilitarians? How do they solve it? Evaluate their solution.

*5. Evaluate Mill's answers to the three objections listed.

6. How can a utilitarian account for justice? Justice looks to the past, to the deed done, while utilitarianism looks to the future, to consequences. Are these compatible? Imagine you are a judge. One defendant has only stolen an apple, but his temperament and threats make him a danger to society. The other has committed first degree murder but is sincerely repentant and has a personality and a life history full of philanthropy, kindness, and altruism. Would utilitarian principles tell you to give the first man a longer jail sentence than the second, even though that is manifestly unjust?

KIERKEGAARD

1. Which of Kierkegaard's three "stages" is innate in us? If only the "aesthetic" is innate rather than learned, how do

we choose to learn to be ethical or religious? Are there also inborn ethical and religious instincts?

2. Is our inability to teach animals to be ethical or religious explained in the same way as our inability to teach them to speak articulate sentences?

3. Why do some people never "graduate" beyond the aesthetic stage, while others do?

4. Classify at least three philosophers, three fictional characters, and three real people into Kierkegaard's three stages.

5. Do you see any other way to classify the "stages on life's way"? Compare them with Kierkegaard's.

6. Could a philosophy that seems to be and claims to be ethical really be only aesthetic? Why or why not?

7. How can Kierkegaard say the aesthete has no "self"?

8. Some thinkers (Hume, Buddha) say there *is* no substantial self. Would this make ethics impossible? Why or why not?

9. One chooses between pleasure and pain (or between interest and boredom) *aesthetically*; one chooses between good and evil *ethically*; and one chooses between belief (faith) and unbelief (or sin) *religiously*; but how does one choose between the aesthetic and the ethical, or between the ethical alone and the religious?

10. Is the choice of atheism a *religious* choice? Is the choice to live aesthetically an *ethical* choice? Explain.

11. In *Either/Or*, Kierkegaard presents the ethical life as rather abstract and boring, at least from the aesthete's point of view. He has Kantian ethics in mind. Is he right? Is he right also about the ethics of Plato or Aristotle?

12. (1) Does a religious believer obey moral principles because he obeys God, or does he obey God because he obeys moral principles? (2) Does a faithful husband obey the commandment against adultery because he loves his wife, because he loves being ethical, or because he loves God? Do these three

options correspond to Kierkegaard's three stages or not? (3) Are these two cases (1) and (2) the same or different?

13. Why doesn't God's command to Abraham to sacrifice his son Isaac make God an immoral, arbitrary tyrant?

NIETZSCHE

1. Is it ironic, accidental, or natural that Kierkegaard and Nietzsche are so similar in personal temperament and yet so opposite in what they love and what they hate?

2. How can one really question "the will to truth"?

3. How would you answer Nietzsche's demand to justify "the will to truth"?

4. What is the meaning of "beyond" in Nietzsche's "beyond good and evil"? "Beyond" in what direction? Why is that direction not simply Nietzsche's concept of "good"? How can it be good to go beyond good?

5. Is there any *positive* point in Nietzsche's hatred of ethics and religion? In Nietzsche's attack on Christian love and compassion as "slave morality"?

6. Does Nietzsche's attack on all Christian values *depend* on his belief in the nonexistence of God? Is it a *necessary* consequence of that belief? Compare Sartre on this.

7. What do you think should be the relationship between "the Apollonian" (reason) and "the Dionysian" (passion)? Why?

8. Is it possible for mankind to become a new species (the "Overman") just by willing it?

9. Can there be spiritual species as well as biological species?

10. Why isn't Nietzsche's worship of "the will to power" simply arbitrary? Can't any value whatsoever be chosen as "self-justifying"? Can anything *justify* calling it "self-justifying"?

11. Modern Western civilization, ever since Bacon, has dedicated itself to "the conquest of nature" by science and technology. Isn't this Nietzsche's "will to power"? If not, why not? If so, so what?

*12. Is Nietzsche (1) right, (2) exaggerated, (3) confused, (4) humanly wicked, or (5) Satanic? Why? Why not the other four?

SARTRE

1. If it is true that most people who agree with Sartre are troubled and unhappy, what does that prove?
2. Do you agree with Dostoevsky that "if God does not exist, everything is permissible" or not? Why?
3. If you agree with that premise, which deduction seems more likely to you: that God does not exist and therefore that everything is permissible, or that not everything is permissible and therefore that God exists? Why?
4. What are some alternative definitions of freedom that contradict Sartre's?
5. Compare "freedom" with "power." Does Sartre do with freedom the same thing Nietzsche does with power?
6. How does one come to Sartre's conclusion that life is "absurd"? How does one avoid it?
7. Is it possible for our choices to *create* moral values? Compare other fields: sports, math, art, politics.
8. Why isn't "There are no wrong choices" self-contradictory? (Isn't it then a wrong choice to say that there are wrong choices?)
9. What causes the difference between Sartre's uncomfortable atheism and the more popular comfortable atheism he criticizes?
10. How effective is the argument toward the end of the chapter to the effect that if Sartre is right, love is impossible? Is this a *reductio ad absurdum* argument?
11. Many people are sitting on the fence about religion. Do you think that reading Sartre would drive more of them into atheism or into religion? Answer the same question regarding Nietzsche.

1. To what extent do you think it is possible to do what the phenomenological method tries to do—namely, to listen to the data of experience without prejudices, premises, or presuppositions?

2. How does one choose between (1) believing that "there are more things in heaven and earth [i.e., in reality] than are dreamt of in your philosophy" (Shakespeare), (2) believing that there are fewer things in reality than are dreamt of in your philosophy (reductionism), and (3) believing that there are the same number of things in reality as are dreamt of in your philosophy (rationalism)?

3. Is reductionism self-contradictory? Must one implicitly claim omniscience in order to be certain that X is only Y—i.e., that there is no dimension of X or example of X or kind of X *anywhere* that is more than Y?

4. Like Plato, Marcel identifies "being" with "goodness" (intrinsic value). Why? What might justify this? What seems to contradict it?

5. Evaluate Marcel's answer to the question of why philosophers have never definitively solved any "mysteries" such as the seven mentioned in paragraph 4.

*6. Does a "mystery" invite or repel investigation? What sort of progress can be made in casting light on "mysteries"? Compare this with the progress of science.

7. How can "fidelity" be "creative" if it obeys rules?

8. Explain how Mark 12:13–17, John 8:3–11, and 1 Kings 3:16–28 are examples of Marcel's "creative fidelity."

1. Can you come up with any other fundamental divisions of "good" besides Hildebrand's three?

2. Can you come up with any ethical principle more fundamental than the "three R principle" of Right Response to Reality?

3. Compare the "will to truth" that Nietzsche questioned (the imperative to live intellectually in the real world, to believe and say that the sky is blue because the sky *is* blue) with Hildebrand's "value response" (the imperative to live morally in the real world, to respond to this value because it is a value that demands your appropriate response to it).

*4. Are there other explanations besides Plato's (what is Plato's explanation, by the way?) and Hildebrand's (what is his explanation, by the way?) as to why we often choose evil? If so, evaluate them.

5. How would Kant criticize Hildebrand's ethics of the heart? How can we be morally responsible for spontaneous acts of compassion or selfishness that do not spring from our reason and free choice but from our "inclinations"?

6. How does Hildebrand synthesize the insights of Kant and Aristotle?

7. Give some examples of emotions that are insights, or intentional, and some examples of emotions that are not.

AYER

1. Ayer, like Hume, deduces his ethics from his epistemology. How? Is this necessary or not? Why?

*2. Does Hume's premise that there are only two kinds of cognitively meaningful propositions ("relations of ideas" and empirical "matters of fact") necessarily result in Ayer's conclusion that ethical propositions are cognitively meaningless? Why or why not?

3. If the answer to question 2 is yes, does it necessarily follow that Ayer's "boo-hoorah theory" is a *reductio ad absurdum* that disproves his and Hume's epistemological premise? Can epistemological or metaphysical theories be refuted by their ethical consequences?

4. Why is the "boo-hoorah theory" obviously absurd? Or is it?

5. If it is so absurd that even Ayer repudiated it, why does it remain so very popular among ordinary people and even intellectuals? If the answer is its "tolerance" and "non-judgmentalism," why do "tolerance" and "non-judgmentalism" appear more important than justice, conscience, or virtue to so many people? If there is no logical defense of it (is there?), then what is the strong motivating force behind it?

6. Total tolerance seems self-contradictory, since it is intolerant of intolerance, and total non-judgmentalism seems self-contradictory because it judges judgmentalism. Is this merely a clever logical sophism or a real refutation? Why?

MOORE

1. If a term is indefinable, does that mean it is cognitively meaningless? If not, why not?

2. Has Moore refuted Plato, Aristotle, Epicurus, Mill, and Kant (par. 2)? Why or why not?

*3. Did Plato make essentially the same point as Moore when he called the good infinite and therefore indefinable in the *Republic*? But Plato gave three meaningful *analogies* for it (the sun, the divided line, and the cave) in the *Republic*; why didn't Moore do the same?

4. Can *you* define "good"?

5. If (1) the good is real, and if (2) it is indefinable, what metaphysical conclusion follows about the nature and extent of what is real? Why do you suppose Moore did not draw this conclusion?

6. Moore assumes that common sense should be a standard for philosophy and should judge philosophies, rather than philosophy being a standard for common sense and judging common sense. Which do you think it should be and why? What would Socrates say about this question?

WITTGENSTEIN

1. Does Wittgenstein mean the same thing by "mystical" as Moore means by "indefinable" or "non-natural?" If not, what is the difference?
2. Is there a position halfway between that of the early Wittgenstein and Ayer on the one hand, and the later Wittgenstein's "mysticism" on the other hand? If not, why not? If so, what would it be?
*3. Why is the "I" or knowing subject "mystical"?
4. Why is existence itself "mystical"?
5. Is beauty "mystical?" How might you try to define it?
6. How can gardening in a monastery be more philosophical than lecturing at Cambridge?

MACINTYRE

1. Evaluate MacIntyre's claim (a) historically and (b) sociologically or psychologically.
2. If MacIntyre is right, what can we do about it?
3. Who do you think is right on this issue (whether the natural moral law can be forgotten): MacIntyre or Aquinas? Why?
4. Evaluate each paragraph of the Aquinas reading.
5. Does the sudden and almost total reversal of opinion on the morality of homosexuality prove MacIntyre's claim?
6. Why is this issue so difficult to argue about and so passionately held on both sides today? Why is this not the case in non-Western or non-modern civilizations?
7. Is a mediating position possible? If so, how?

Appendix II:
Ten Methods
for Writing Essays

Great philosophers often offer new *methods* of thinking and of expressing thoughts, and these methods are often very useful no matter what the *content* of those thoughts might be. They do not decide what ideas are true or false, but they organize our ideas and arguments more clearly. There are a number of methods suggested by different philosophers (some of them not in this book) that you might look into and use yourself, for instance:

1. Descartes' four rules of the method of universal doubt;
2. Hegel's "dialectic" of thesis, antithesis, and higher synthesis;
3. Kierkegaard's method of "indirect communication," adopting alternative points of view, perspectives, personas, or sets of fundamental categories;
4. Husserl's and Hildebrand's method of phenomenology (essentially, carefully gathering all the data of ordinary experience that is relevant before categorizing, judging, or arguing about it);
5. G.E. Moore's method of extremely careful analysis of exactly what you mean by your language and how it relates to what

ordinary people commonsensically mean by their ordinary language;

6. a more free-flowing personal journal, diary, or autobiographical account of how you learned what you think is some wisdom or unlearned what you think is some error, perhaps along the lines of Augustine's *Confessions*. This need not be, but can be, written as a letter to God and in the presence of the all-knowing God, if you believe in such a God, as Augustine did, in order to radically enhance your honesty.

You can further research these methods by reading the philosophers who invented them and seeing how they practiced them, thus becoming apprentices. There is nothing servile, passive, or uncritical about imitation of a master; it is called apprenticeship, and it is in fact the way beginners learn just about everything in the world.

Four of the methods that my students and I have often found very useful are:

1. the Socratic dialogue, as written by Plato;
2. the live Socratic debate;
3. the use of Aristotelian logic to organize the progression of your thoughts; and
4. the *Summa*-style "article," as practiced by St. Thomas Aquinas.

Following is some advice on these last four methods, from the author's *Socratic Logic*.

Appendix III:
How to
Write a Socratic Dialogue

I have written and published about a dozen full-length books of Socratic dialogues, and judging by reader reactions, they are among the most successful and appreciated of my ninety-odd published books. So I want to spread the secret (which is no secret at all, as far as I can see).

Like most philosophy students, I loved reading Plato and found the dramatic form of dialogue much more engaging than the monologue. A monologue is more likely to commit the one unforgivable sin of any writer—boring the reader—because it has only one voice, it is impersonal, and it usually lacks drama. I wondered why so few other philosophers copied Plato's dialogue form and why, even when they did, the dialogues were not really Socratic. I still don't know. (Augustine's *On the Teacher* and Berkeley's *Three Dialogues Between Hylas and Philonous* are the only two lasting philosophical classics I know in dialogue form, unless you count Boethius' *The Consolation of Philosophy* as a dialogue too.)

No one knows how close Plato's Socrates is to the actual historical Socrates, but Plato surely included *some* invented fiction, however closely based on Socrates' historical character; so I could think of no reason why we today could not extend the historical figure of Socrates through our own imagination. I asked many people why we couldn't, but no one gave me an answer. So I tried a simple experiment, with my students as the guinea pigs.

I always introduce students to philosophy first through Socrates, and I encourage original essays, so I suggested that the students write their essays by imitating Plato's form and writing Socratic dialogues. Many tried it, and almost all succeeded, both by their own estimation and by mine. If students can do it, why can't teachers? I couldn't imagine why not. So to find out why it can't be done, I did it. And the answer is simply that there is *no* reason why it can't be done! Furthermore, I think I can even give at least a few pieces of pretty obvious and commonsensical advice to others now about *how* to do it. Here they are:

POINTS OF PERSONAL ADVICE TO THE WRITER

1. As with most enterprises, the first and necessary step is "Begin!" "Just do it." "Try." For "well begun is half done" (ancient Greek proverb) and "whatever is worth doing, is worth doing badly" (G.K. Chesterton).
2. Don't be afraid to imitate. Apprenticeship by imitation was the primary method of teaching almost anything (and it worked!) until the modern cult of individuality and originality. You can never be as creative or original by trying to be original as you can by forgetting all about originality and just "doing your thing." And if anyone is imitable and worth imitating, it's Socrates.
3. So immerse yourself in Socrates. Read all of Plato's earlier dialogues, up to the *Republic*, book 1. In the later dialogues, beginning with books 2–10 of the *Republic*, the personality of Socrates recedes and Plato the professor emerges. He may be an excellent professor and a great philosopher, and his system may be a valid extension of Socrates' beginnings, but he's just

not Socrates, as St. Paul may be a profoundly wise and great Christian, but he's just not Jesus.

4. Instinctive and inward imitation is better than contrived and external imitation. Let the *spirit* of Socrates get under your skin, so that you can use your imagination and ask yourself: What would the real, historical Socrates have said here? Socrates' method is both personal and impersonally logical. Learn both aspects, but don't neglect the inner spirit.

5. There are two ways to write a Socratic dialogue: (a) You can simply use your imagination, be Socrates and his dialogue partner (let us call him "O" for "other"), and let the argument and the two personalities carry you wherever they naturally go, like a river; or (b) you can make a logical map of the argument before you begin and add the dramatic and personal dimension to it as you write. If (b) proves too un-Socratic and artificial, try (a). If (a) proves too unstructured, use (b) at least for a while. After some practice with (b), you may be able to transition to (a).

6. Whether you use (a) or (b) above, you must know the structures of logic, naturally and instinctively.

7. In the process of arguing, use the rules for Socratic debate in the next section, "How to Have a Socratic Debate."

POINTS OF ADVICE IN CONSTRUCTING THE DRAMATIC CHARACTER OF SOCRATES

1. Confine yourself to only two characters, Socrates and "O." Perhaps later you can add other characters, as Plato does, but even then each should take his turn; do not put three or more people into the conversation at once (except perhaps very briefly). If you do, that will loosen its logical structure, and *argument* will turn into *conversation*.

2. The initial question should arise naturally from an ordinary situation or conversation. It should not be artificial or imposed but arise from "O's" interests.

3. Like Plato, you might want to add the little trick of placing a veiled clue to the central point of the dialogue in the very first line.

4. Socrates asks the questions rather than giving the answers (except in response to "O's" questions). Remember, Socrates is not a preacher. (This is easy to understand but surprisingly hard to obey.)

5. There is always an ironic contrast between Socrates' knowing that he doesn't know and "O's" not knowing that he doesn't know. The one who seems to know, doesn't; and the one who seems not to know, does. The one who seems to be the student (Socrates) is really the teacher, and vice versa.

6. This irony may emerge in the interaction between the characters if "O" is a bit arrogant—in which case Socrates gets a chance to use his (always light and subtle) ironic wit and humor. But "O" should never be oversimplified, unfairly treated, put down, or preached at—and neither should the reader.

7. The personal, psychological struggle is as much a part of the Socratic dialogue as the struggle of ideas. A Socratic dialogue is a form of spiritual warfare, therapy, or doctoring to the spirit of the student. Yet paradoxically, it is for this reason that you must avoid direct personal confrontation and let the *argument* always be the object of attention. Socrates sees himself and "O" not as a winner and a loser but as two scientists mutually seeking the truth by testing two alternative hypotheses. Whichever one finds the truth, both are winners.

8. Sometimes "O" is convinced and converted in mind by the argument and sometimes not, depending on his personality as well as his intelligence.

9. Socrates' goal is always ultimately somehow moral (though this is not always apparent at first). For he has only one lifetime, and it is too precious to waste on issues that are not somehow connected to the most important purpose of human life, becoming more wise and virtuous.

10. Socrates' aim is not to harm but to help "O." Sometimes this involves shame, but it never involves a conflict of interests—at least not from Socrates' point of view. "O" may or may not understand this, but Socrates, like Jesus, is altruistic in his very offensiveness. He believes, as Aquinas says, that there is no greater act of charity one can do to his neighbor than to lead him to the truth. Socratic dialogue is ultimately (non-religious) missionary work.

POINTS OF ADVICE ABOUT THE LOGICAL METHOD

1. The question must be defined early on.
2. The question should be formulated disjunctively so that it has only two possible answers. Otherwise, an infinite number of arguments, and of dialogues, will be necessary. In the *Republic*, for example, the question "What is justice?" quickly becomes "Is justice the interest of the stronger or not?" and "Is justice always more profitable than injustice or not?"
3. Potentially ambiguous terms must be defined by mutual agreement.
4. Like a psychoanalyst, Socrates does not give his opinion unless it is demanded but rather asks "O" what *he* believes.
5. Once he gets an answer from "O," Socrates may now use one or more of the following four logical strategies:
    a. Ask "O" *why* he believes this and examine "O's" argument, looking for an ambiguous term, a false premise, or a logical fallacy; or
    b. trace "O's" premises back to further premises, either by *showing* what missing premises "O's" enthymemes (arguments with a premise implied but not expressed) must presuppose or else *asking* "O" to prove his premises and then examining that proof; or
    c. draw out the *consequences* of "O's" belief in a (usually multi-step) *reductio ad absurdum* (look it up!); or

    d. construct an argument whose conclusion will be the contradictory of "O's" belief. If Socrates does this, his argument should begin well "upstream" from the falls where "O" will come to grief. It should usually be a long, linear chain argument, whose first premise "O" will agree to, like a man who puts his boat into a calm, inviting river upstream and then finds that the river takes him downstream to rapids and waterfalls—and sinking. However, sometimes this argument is short, often an argument by analogy.

6. After the "sinking" the dialogue can end or begin again with another attempt.

7. Socrates rarely uses many arguments for the same conclusion, preferring one very sure and carefully worked-out argument rather than a larger number of weaker arguments that need reinforcements. When he does use a number of cumulative arguments (e.g., in the *Phaedo* to prove the immortality of the soul), they are usually surprisingly unconvincing. (Contrast Plato's more convincing single argument for immortality in the Republic, book 10.)

8. The dialogue ends either with closure and proof (as in the *Republic*) or not (as in the *Meno*). If with closure, "O" may accept this (as in the *Republic*) or not (as in the *Gorgias*). If the dialogue does not end with closure, a better answer may be suggested (as in the *Meno*) or it may not (as in the *Euthyphro*).

9. If Socrates interacts with modern people, remember that he is not a typically modern person—in his personality, in his assumptions, in his style of speech, or in his unlimited patience.

Appendix IV:
How to
Have a Socratic Debate

The Middle Ages "institutionalized" two forms of Socratic debate. One was the "Scholastic Disposition," an elaborate, demanding, and (to modern minds) artificial form. The subject was usually a highly technical philosophical or theological question, and the format was confined to strictly labeled syllogistic forms. The other was the written form of the "articles" in a *Summa*, a collection of abbreviated summaries of such a disputation, the most famous of which was the *Summa theologiae* of St. Thomas Aquinas.

Neither form is ideal for debate today without revision, for the logic is too demandingly formal and technical, but it is still a useful format for a short summary (see the last section of this Appendix). The Scholastic Disputation is too long (they often lasted for half a day), and the *Summa* article too short (it is often only one page or less). But the basic principles that governed such debates can be summarized and used to good effect in a modern, more informal (and thus more Socratic) debate, as I have done below.

Some of these rules were explicitly stated, some assumed and implied, by medieval debaters. The reader will notice the similarity of many of the following points to those that we have already listed as governing a Socratic dialogue; for in a sense both the Scholastic Disputation and the *Summa* were systematizations of the Socratic dialogue, although the Socratic debate is much looser and more unpredictable.

SOME RULES ABOUT ATTITUDES AND PRESUPPOSITIONS:

1. Total honesty is presupposed. This means (a) that the aim of both parties must be simply to seek and find the truth; (b) that this truth is *the* truth, not "my" truth or "your" truth—i.e., objective and universal truth; and (c) that personal victory or defeat should be purely incidental and not the goal aimed at. (This will be difficult for you. What does that tell you about yourself?)
2. Neither party to the debate should be either a skeptic (who believes that no one can hope to know anything) or a personal dogmatist (who believes that he already knows it all). A skeptic thinks he can't be right, and a dogmatist thinks he can't be wrong. Neither has a reason to inquire.
3. Both the fear of reason (which Socrates calls "misology" in the *Phaedo*) and scorn of anything other than pure reason ("rationalism" in the worst, narrowest sense) are rejected at the outset.

SOME RULES ABOUT PROTOCOL AND PROCEDURES:

1. Reasons must always be given when asked for. "Why?" is always a legitimate question.
2. "Follow the argument wherever it goes." Reason is the common master. The two debaters are like rafts, and the argument is like a river.
3. The river has both calm and turbulent parts and perhaps rocks and waterfalls. But the aim is to find the sea of truth, not to tip your opponent's raft over.

4. Always listen before you respond so that you respond to what was actually said. In fact, no one has the right to respond to his opponent's argument until he has first restated that argument in his own words (to prove that he understands the meaning, not just the words), to his opponent's satisfaction. (That often takes more time than you think it will.)

5. The order must always be: first, data (what, exactly, was actually said?); then, interpretation of the data (what the speaker means, not what the hearer would have meant); then, evaluation and argument (is he right or wrong?). This might be called "constructionism," for it is in explicit contradiction to the method that calls itself "deconstructionism," perhaps the most polar opposite to a Socratic debate in the entire history of philosophy.

6. Two formats are possible: (a) In the formal one, each debater is given a set amount of time to state, and his opponent to try to refute, his argument, turn by turn. For example, A summarizes his argument in five minutes, then B has five minutes to respond, then A has five minutes to respond to B, then B gets another five minutes, etc. (b) In the informal format, preset time structures are not imposed.

7. Whether the time is explicitly counted and monitored or not, in both formats each debater must be given approximately equal time or at least enough time to satisfy him and his need to explain himself.

8. The debate will usually work better with an impartial moderator, but it can sometimes work without one, if both parties adhere conscientiously to all the rules. Any two people can start a debate club, or a "Saint Socrates Society." Try it! You might begin a quiet revolution.

SOME RULES ABOUT ARGUING
LOGICALLY

1. Arguments must be stated explicitly, preferably (though not necessarily) in syllogistic form.

2. When confronted by an argument, there are *only* four legitimate responses:

    a. "I do not accept your conclusion because you have used a term ambiguously (and I will point out which term that is and show how you have used it ambiguously)"; or

    b. "I do not accept your conclusion because you have assumed a false premise (and I will show [1] which premise it is, [2] why it is logically necessary for you to assume it, and [3] why it is false)"; or

    c. "I do not accept your conclusion because your argument contains a logical fallacy (and I will point out this fallacy in your argument)";

    d. "I can find no ambiguous term, false premise, or logical fallacy in your argument, therefore I must accept your conclusion as true, since I am an honest, intelligent, open-minded seeker of objective truth rather than a dishonest, stupid, closed-minded seeker of personal victory."

    There is no fifth option, "I can find none of these three errors in your argument; you have proved your conclusion to be true; but I do not accept it. I will not tell you why. Instead, this conclusion you have proved to be objectively true I will label 'your' truth, as I hug 'my' truth to myself like an auto-erotic intellectual security blanket."

3. When your opponent finds an ambiguously used term, you must redefine it and reword your argument without ambiguity or else abandon your argument and find another one. When he claims to find a false premise, you must prove that it is not false or else that you do not need to assume this

premise. When he claims to find a logical fallacy, you must show how he has misunderstood the logic of your argument or else reword your argument to avoid the fallacy.

4. Do not leave arguments "hanging." Do not respond to his argument proving X simply by an argument proving non-X. Refute his argument, not just his conclusion.

5. One long, linear, many-step argument is preferable to many cumulative arguments because this "backs up" the discussion onto more and more fundamental premises, so that even if no one "wins" the debate, both see more clearly the more basic reasons behind their disagreement.

6. Be honest enough to change your mind if your opponent convinces you. Remember, no one loses a Socratic debate except ignorance, and no one wins except truth. If no one finds truth, both lose. If one finds it, both win.

These many points of advice will seem very complex and difficult if you have no experience of reading Socratic dialogues but surprisingly simple, easy, and obvious if you have.

Appendix V:
How to Write a Logical Essay
Using Aristotelian Logic

Students are required to write essays throughout their educational career. This ability can even determine whether or not you get into a good college or graduate school, or get good enough grades to stay in. The simple, three acts-of-the-mind structure of Socratic-Aristotelian logic gives us an ideal simplified form for writing an effective, clear, and persuasive essay.

What follows is certainly not the *only* good way to write a persuasive essay. But it is a simple and effective way, and many intelligent students today have never been taught even this simple form. That is why it may seem at first artificial and confining or "picky" and overstrict. However, following this seven-step guideline in each detail can make a tremendous difference: the difference between a vague, weak, rambling, disordered, confusing, and therefore non-persuasive essay, and a sharp, strong, economical, orderly, clear, and convincing one.

It will feel rigid at first, but rigid forms are necessary for beginners in every field. Aspiring poets should first learn to write sonnets before writing free verse. Pianists must first master scales and chords before Bach's two-part Inventions. Babies need walkers, and the lame need crutches, and sinners need "organized religion."

The principles below can apply to argumentative essays of any length but especially to a medium-length essay in the neighborhood of 3–6 pages.

1. Choose a good topic. A good topic for a logical essay has all three of the following qualities:
    a. It is *controversial*—that is, argued-about. "War is painful" is not controversial; "all wars are unjust" is. "Man is mortal" is not controversial; "man can be made immortal" is.
    b. It is *specific*. "Philosophers have helped humanity" is not specific; "Aristotle's philosophy helped the progress of science more than Descartes' philosophy did" is specific.
    c. It is an *either/or*: a single question with only two possible answers, as in formal debates. "What is God?" is not a good topic. "Is God unchanging?" is.
2. Explain the importance of your question to motivate the reader's interest. What *difference* is made by answering it in one way versus the other way?
3. Give your answer (thesis, conclusion). This is the "point" of your whole essay. This tends to come at the end in a Socratic dialogue, but it should usually be "up front" and come at the beginning in an essay.
4. Define your terms. Terms need defining if they are:
    a. *ambiguous* (can be taken in two or more different senses); or
    b. *obscure or technical* to some readers; or
    c. *controversial* (i.e., imply a presupposition that not everyone agrees with, like "anti-life" or "anti-choice" in an essay on abortion. Avoid such terms in an essay unless you need them and will defend them).

5. Prove your thesis. Give one or more *reasons* (arguments) for it. These reasons will be either *inductive* (from specific examples) or *deductive* (from a general principle).

    If they are deductive, your reasons will be either *linear* (A, therefore B, therefore C, therefore D) or *cumulative* (D is true because of A, and also because of B, and also because of C).

    Each of your arguments should have:

    a. no ambiguous terms;

    b. no false premises; and

    c. no logical fallacies (i.e., the conclusion should follow necessarily from the premises).

6. Summarize and then answer the strongest and most commonly given arguments for the opposite position. (Remember, since you formulated your thesis in an either/or, yes-or-no form, there are only two possible answers to your question.)

    To refute an argument, you do not merely find a counter-argument to prove the opposite conclusion, but you must:

    a. first summarize the argument honestly and fairly;

    b. then analyze (take apart) the argument and explain what is wrong with it. That is, you must find and show the presence of one of the only three things that can go wrong with an argument:

        i. a term used ambiguously (Which term? Distinguish its two meanings. Show how it has changed its meaning in the course of your opponent's argument.); or

        ii. a false premise (Which premise? Is it stated or implied? If implied, prove that it is necessarily implied. Whether stated or implied, show that it is false; give reasons for disagreeing with it.); or

        iii. a logical fallacy. (Which fallacy? Show that the
conclusion does not logically follow from the
premises.)

7. To be maximally complete and fair, add one more step:
anticipate and answer objections.

    a. Imagine the strongest way your opponent would try to
refute *your* arguments (the ones that you gave in part
5) in one of the three ways above, and then

    b. defend your argument against these criticisms.

Appendix VI:
How to
Write a *Summa* Article

A *Summa* article is a condensation of another great philosophical form, the Socratic dialogue. The literary form of the Socratic dialogue emerged in Plato's hands from the actual practice of Socrates in *lived* dialogue; and the format of the medieval *Summa* article emerged, especially in the work of St. Thomas Aquinas, from actual debates or "Scholastic Disputations," which were something like formalized, systematized Socratic dialogues.

The main reason the *Summa* article is unpopular today, I think, is that it "feels" very different to modern man than it did to medieval man. I have described it, above, as a short, systematic summary of a Socratic dialogue; but most moderns "feel" a very different spirit in it than they feel in Socrates. They feel an artificial, stuffy, self-satisfied "gotcha!"; they feel it is really a monologue instead of a dialogue; and they feel an arrogance rather than a humility.

If this is your feeling, my only answer is that that feeling is indeed telling—about you, but not about Aquinas or about his format. Why, one might as well accuse a physicist's equations or a detective's fingerprinting of being "arrogant." It is, indeed, impersonal and scientific and objective. But surely that is part of *humility*, while the demand to "share your own feelings" all the time is part of pride and self-importance.

Each article begins by formulating in its title a single question in such a way that only two answers are possible: yes or no. St. Thomas does this, not because he thinks philosophy or theology is as simple as a true/false exam, but because he wants to make an issue finite and decidable, just as debaters do in formulating their "resolution." There are an indefinite number of possible answers to a question like "What is God?" If he had formulated his questions that way, the *Summa* might be four million pages long instead of four thousand. Instead, he asks, for example, "Whether God Is a Body?" It is possible to decide and demonstrate that one of the two possible answers (yes) is false and therefore that the other (no) is true.

By the way, there is no reason that the *Summa* article should be confined to theological content. It is simply a logical form that is neutral to content.

Each article has five structural parts. First, the question is formulated in a yes-or-no format, as explained above, beginning with the word "Whether" (*Utrum*).

Second, St. Thomas lists a number of objections (usually at least three) to the answer he will give. The objections are apparent proofs of this opposite answer, the other side to the debate. These objections begin with the formula: "It seems that . . ." (*Oportet*). The objections are to be taken seriously, as *apparent* truth. One who is seeking the strongest possible arguments *against* any idea of St. Thomas will rarely find any stronger ones, any more strongly argued, than those in St. Thomas himself. He is extremely fair to all his opponents.

Third, St. Thomas indicates his own position with the formula "On the contrary" (*Sed contra*). This is not his strongest proof; in fact, sometimes it is not a proof at all, but only a reminder that authoritative sources teach his position. When it is an argument, it is single, brief, and an "argument from authority"—i.e., its premise (in St. Thomas) is from Scripture, the Fathers of the Church, or recognized wise men. The medievals well knew their own maxim that "the argument from (merely human) authority is the weakest of all arguments" (see *Summa theologiae* 1.1.8 obj. 2). But they also believed in doing their homework and in learning from their ancestors—two habits we would do well to cultivate today.

The fourth part, "I answer that" (*Respondeo dicens*), is the body of the article. In it, St. Thomas proves his own position, often adding necessary background explanations and making needed definitions and distinctions along the way. The easiest (but not the most exciting) way to read a *Summa* article is to read this part first.

Fifth and finally, each objection must be addressed and answered, not merely by an argument to prove the opposite conclusion, for that has already been done in the body of the article, but by explaining where and how the objection went wrong—i.e., by distinguishing the truth from the falsity in the objection, usually by distinguishing two meanings of one of the objector's terms.

No one of these five steps can be omitted if we want to have good grounds for settling a controverted question. If our question is vaguely or confusedly formulated, our answer will be too. If we do not consider opposing views, we spar without a partner and paw the air. If we do not do our homework, we only skim the shallows of ourselves. If we do not prove our thesis, we are dogmatic, not critical. And if we do not understand and refute our opponents, we are left with nagging uncertainty that we have missed something and not really ended the contest.

Like Socratic dialogue for Plato, this medieval method of philosophizing was very fruitful in its own day—and then subsequently neglected, especially in our day. That is one of the unsolved mysteries of Western thought. Surely both the Socratic and the Thomistic methodological trees can still bear much good fruit. Perhaps what stands in the way is our craze for originality and our proud refusal to be anyone's apprentice. I for one would be very happy to be Aquinas' apprentice, or Socrates'.[1]

The format is easily misused, since *corruptio optimi pessima* (the corruption of the best things are the worst things). Some of its tempting abuses are the following:

1. It is not a private language designed to distinguish professionals from amateurs, or scholars from non-scholars, or the unusually bright from the ordinary. It is natural, simple, and commonsensical. It is addressed to ordinary people. Remember, Aquinas wrote the *Summa theologiae* "for beginners."

2. It is not simplistic, just summary. The topics are typically dealt with very briefly, and they demand and reward much longer, more complex, more detailed, and more nuanced treatment. For instance, Aquinas himself used twenty-one paragraphs in the *Summa contra Gentiles*, which did *not* use the "article" format, to treat the first of his famous "five ways" of demonstrating the existence of God and took only one paragraph to summarize it in the *Summa theologiae*, which did use this method.

3. It is not a "handbook" of arguments to use as weapons to win debates with, like an outline of "proof texts" from the Bible for Fundamentalists to hit unbelievers on the head with. These rigid arguments are to be used flexibly, as a rigid sword is to be swung creatively.

4. And the swordsman's enemies here are not debate opponents. Like a Socratic dialogue, a *Summa* article is not a civil war between two opponents but a joint raid against the common enemies of confusion, ignorance, and error, using the

---

1. In addition to a dozen Socratic dialogues, in which Socrates meets Descartes, Hume, Kant, Kierkegaard, Marx, Freud, Sartre, Machiavelli, and Jesus, I've tried the *Summa* format for 110 controversial philosophical questions in *Summa Philosophica* (all published by St. Augustine's Press).

common weapons of the common master, reason. ("Reason" means "the *three* acts of the mind": [a] understanding clearly *what* a thing is, [b] knowing and judging truly *that* it is, and [c] reasoning rightly to prove *why* it is.)

5. The rigidity of the form does not entail or condone mental rigidity or a dogmatic attitude. There is more than one way to skin a cat.

Since the reader may still have doubts and objections against the possibility of using the *Summa* article format for philosophy today, some of these objections may be stated and answered as follows:

Objection 1: The Thomistic, Scholastic *format* implicitly presupposes a Thomistic, Scholastic *content*. This limits the method to use by Thomists.

Reply: Format is connected to content only accidentally and historically; it can easily be abstracted from content. Similarly, one can write a Socratic dialogue to argue for any philosophical position, including anti-Socratic, anti-Platonic positions.

Objection 2: The Scholastic format lends itself to misuse as a quasi-mathematical system, impersonal and automatic, like an encyclopedia, a handbook, or a self-playing "player piano" instead of an instrument played differently by different players.

Reply: This, too, is an accidental misuse. *Abusus non tollit usum* ("The abuse does not take away the use"). Because format can be abstracted from content (Reply to Objection 1), it can be employed rightly or wrongly, like any tool or power.

Objection 3: The format is appropriate to the Middle Ages but not to today. It is not a mere historical accident that this format has totally disappeared from serious philosophy today. "You can't turn back the clock."

Reply: Chesterton answers that cliché in three simple words: "Yes you can." A clock is a human invention, and when it keeps bad time, it can and should be turned back. It is not our master but our servant. The objection assumes that history is destiny. If the Socratic dialogue format can be resuscitated, there is no reason why the *Summa* article format cannot.

Objection 4: The search for a neat, closed system in philosophy is a wild goose chase. Knowledge is open and evolving, and so is wisdom. It is also always limited and perspectival.

Reply: This is true. But a *Summa* is not a system, and certainly not a closed system. It is ordered but open, an incomplete summary of incomplete knowledge. Aquinas himself asserted that we can never have complete knowledge of the essence of anything, even a flea.